MW00364908

charles HANDY

© Elizabeth Handy Portraits

ROBERT HELLER

A Dorling Kindersley Book

LONDON, NEW YORK, SYDNEY, DELHI, PARIS,
MUNICH & JOHANNESBURG

Managing Editor Adèle Hayward
Senior Art Editor Jamie Hanson
DTP Designer Julian Dams
Production Controller Michelle Thomas

Senior Managing Editor Stephanie Jackson
Senior Managing Art Editor Nigel Duffield
US Editor Gary Werner

Produced for Dorling Kindersley by
Grant Laing Partnership
48 Brockwell Park Gardens,
London SE24 9BJ
Managing Editor Jane Laing
Project Editor Helen Ridge
Managing Art Editor Steve Wilson

First American Edition, 2001
00 01 02 03 04 05 10 9 8 7 6 5 4 3 2 1

Published in the United States by
Dorling Kindersley Publishing, Inc.
95 Madison Avenue
New York, New York 10016

Cataloging-in-Publication Data is available from the Library of Congress

ISBN 0-7894-7158-2
Reproduced by Colourpath, London
Printed in Hong Kong by Wing King Tong

see our complete catalog at
www.dk.com

Author's Acknowledgments
The many sources for this book have been acknowledged in the text, but I must now express my great debt to everybody, above all to the Mastermind himself. Nor would the book exist but for the inspiration and effort of the excellent Dorling Kindersley team – to whom my warm thanks.

Packager's Acknowledgments
Grant Laing Partnership would like to thank the following for their help and participation:
Index Kay Ollerenshaw
Picture Research Andy Sansom

Picture Credits
The publisher would like to thank the following for their kind permission to reproduce the following photographs:
AKG London: Erich Lessing 30; **Corbis UK Ltd:** Bettmann 17; **Garden Picture Library:** Ros Wickham 50; **Elizabeth Handy Portraits: 1, 4, 9, 13, 66, 73**; **Rex Features:** R Laurance 60; **Tony Stone Images:** Wayne Eastep 87; Chris Everard 88; George Grigoriou 14; Aldo Torelli 65

Front jacket: **Elizabeth Handy Portraits**

Contents

Prophet of a new order

Charles Handy is the prophet of a new order, not only in management, but in society at large. The breadth of his vision, together with his imagination and his images, explains the wide popularity of his books. Metaphors like the "portfolio career," "the Inside-out Doughnut," and "the Shamrock Organization" have passed into the language of management. They portray some of the key developments that are changing the ways in which organizations and people work. Handy's penetrating, practical, insightful knowledge of what actually goes on in organizations lends force to his predictions of how and why they will go on changing. His moral philosophy makes the case for why these changes are not only inevitable, but ethical. Handy does not argue (as he once did) that perfect solutions are possible. Rather, he teaches that organizations and people have to learn to live with compromise, discontinuity, inconsistency, and paradox. His prophecies, foretelling the decline of the traditional organization, the traditional job, and the traditional working life, have to a considerable extent already come true.

Robert Heller

Biography

Charles Handy was born in 1932 in Kildare, Ireland, to an ecclesiastical family: his father was the local archdeacon. Although his career has largely revolved around business management, Handy has also been influenced by his religious upbringing and beliefs. There is a discernible and important moral vein in his writings on management and organizations.

The works that won him an international reputation were founded on a not especially successful career in business. After leaving Oriel College, Oxford, with a first-class honors degree in "Greats," Handy crossed the Atlantic to Boston, to study at the Massachusetts Institute of Technology's Sloan School of Management. On his return from the US, Handy worked for two mighty multinationals: Royal Dutch Shell (in the marketing and personnel divisions) and the Anglo-American Corporation, the mining conglomerate (as an economist). He was drawn toward the academic world, however, joining the brand-new London Business School in 1967. He become a professor in 1972 and held his chair until 1994.

Even though, by his own account, he found his career at Shell stultifying, Handy stayed for the best part of a decade, working as a marketing executive at home and abroad. The experiences at the oil company, however disappointing, provided plenty of material for his later writings. His stint with the Anglo-American Corporation was much briefer – a year or so – and generated less grist for what was to become a highly productive mill. Starting with *Understanding Organizations*, published in 1976, Handy had written 10 books by 1995, when *Beyond Certainty* appeared.

His first book, while mainly descriptive, contained some original ideas, which were then fully developed in *Gods of Management*, published in 1978. This was a characteristic Handy title, ambiguous and allusive. The titles of *The Empty Raincoat* (1994) and *Waiting for the Mountain to Move* (1995) likewise force the browser to guess at what lies within. The content, however, is never ambiguous, even though it typically mixes management theory, real-life anecdotes, sociological insights, moral observations, and ethical conclusions. The mix has been very attractive to readers on both sides of the Atlantic, and most of Handy's books are still in print.

Because of his combined interest in business management and religion, Handy was a natural choice for the post of warden of St. George's House at Windsor Castle in England. The purpose of this private study and conference center, where Handy served as warden from 1977 to 1981, is to bridge the gap between God and mammon by concentrating on social ethics and values. Handy also broadcasts regularly on *Thought for the Day*, BBC Radio 4's religious and philosophical spot on the *Today* program, and he has published a collection of those thoughts.

His views on management are always firmly rooted in reason, experience (his own and that of others), and study. In 1987, Handy was asked to conduct a comprehensive examination of management development in the US, Japan, Britain, and Europe. This added still more to the profound store of knowledge that was especially evident in *Understanding Organizations*. His work as an executive and academic has also been influenced by a considerable amount of consulting work for a wide range of organizations. Many of these are nonprofit operations – in education, health, government, and the voluntary sector.

As Handy developed his ideas on the nature and behavior of organizations, all these various influences came into play, together with original ideas on human life and needs. Unlike many management writers, he shows real concern for the health of society and the individual. This concern runs at least as deep as his interest in improving the effectiveness of business. Not surprisingly, he is himself a dedicated individualist; he likes to be described as an "independent" writer, teacher, and broadcaster.

Practicing what he preaches

Handy does not just generate ideas: he lives them. He has used his own life as a test bed for his prophetic ideas on the new ways of organizing a satisfying balance of work and recreation, with his wife Elizabeth acting as a full partner in the enterprise. They married in 1962 and have a son and daughter. Moving between three homes, in London, Norfolk in England, and Chianti in Italy, they lead a highly organized life in which both can pursue their work: Liz Handy is a portrait photographer, and Handy takes pains to ensure that her work is allotted adequate time.

His own work fits the pattern of the "portfolio career," a growing phenomenon, which he was the first to describe. Treating his various occupations as you might stocks in a portfolio, Handy seeks to optimize the return, not only in financial rewards, but in personal satisfaction and contribution to society. In this, Handy is only practicing what he preaches, which is not always true of prophets – and almost became untrue of him. "I was writing books saying people should get the hell out of organizations at the age of 50," he told *The New York Times*, "and I realized I was 49 and in an organization."

So Handy left St. George's House and started filling his self-employed portfolio. From 1986 to 1988 that included chairing Britain's Royal Society for the Encouragement of Arts, Manufacture, and Commerce. But otherwise he has avoided institutions as his life follows the S-shaped "Sigmoid Curve" (see p. 73), which he thinks is basic to all human life, including that of organizations. Even his marriage has tested this theory. Handy believes that marriages break down because couples wait until "point B" on the downward swing of the Curve before acting:

Working partnership
Charles and Elizabeth Handy live what Handy has termed "a portfolio life," balancing their skills and their time to make the most of their independent careers.

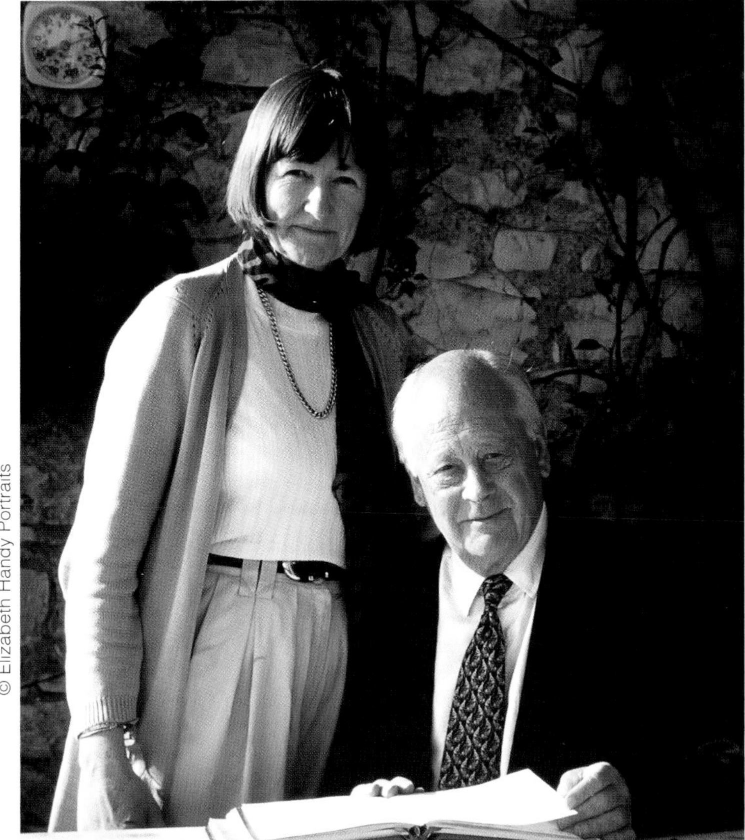

"Too often, couples cling on to their old habits and contracts for too long.... They find other partners. On the other hand, I sometimes like to say, teasingly, that I am on my second marriage – but with the same partner, which makes it less expensive.... I would not deny, however, that [it] was difficult as we struggled to keep what was best in our past while we experimented with the new."

The result of their experiments is a most remarkable lifestyle. "We divided our work roles together," he says, "and then we divided up our time in a very organized way." As his son Scott describes it: "My parents spend 100 days a year working, 100 writing, 100 for charity and 65 on vacation. Six months of the year, my mother decides where they are going to be, and six months of the year, he decides – I think they've been apart for nine days of their marriage."

Handy adds that "having divided up our work roles, our time, and our places, we also have different categories of work that we devote specific time to" – that is, Handy will only accept public engagements that take place during the winter months, while his wife takes on photographic jobs only from March to October. *The New York Times* commented that Handy sounds as if he is talking about "a new management project, not a marriage." But the marriage is very much a working arrangement. Liz Handy "accompanies her husband on trips, handles his calendar, fields his calls, negotiates his contracts, and decides whom it is worthwhile for him to see."

Handy is convinced that other people will have to learn the art of self-management. "We'll all leave organizations earlier, and we're all likely to have 30 years on our own now. So I believe that from the age of 50 onward, every man and woman will have to learn to manage their own life."

"If we could understand... the ways in which individuals were motivated we could influence them by changing the components of that motivation process." *Understanding Organizations*

Handy found the bookstores "crammed with volumes of varying size and quality, directed at the practicing executive, full of the latest nostrums or gimmicks." He contends that witch-doctoring is no good substitute for "old-fashioned commonsense." Whatever managers are taught much can only be learned in the school of experience.

Handy confidently asserted in 1998 that this explained why his book was still "essential reading for anyone interested in organizations and how to make them work better." His "guidebook," as he called it, was "larded... with anecdotes and examples from my own and others' experience." The larding (embellishing) emphasized that useful theory must be grounded in reality. But Handy also wanted to make his book pleasurable to read, "even fun at times." In that way, the book defined not only Handy's area of contribution, but his distinctive, accessible, and diverting style.

1

Sorting out the cultures

How most of the world's large organizations are structured like an ancient Greek temple • Understanding the way organizations work • **The four remedies that combat role stress** • Eight ways in which management groups can go wrong • **Matching the organization's structure to its culture** • Distinguishing the four types of culture – power, role, task, and individual • **Why the chosen responses of most organizations will not work in future** • The changing patterns of work and organizations

Charles Handy's iconoclastic and pathfinding theories all developed out of his first book, *Understanding Organizations*, which was published in 1976. Neither challenging nor heretical, it is a work of scholarship, a *tour de force*, but not recognizably the work of the free-thinking radical that Handy was to become only a couple of years after that first publication. It is as if he needed to immerse himself in the conventions of organizations and in the writings of other management gurus before reaching the conclusion that both organizations and their existing theorists were inadequate.

This almost encyclopedic exercise was to reach its climax in the development of a powerful, unscientific theory about the role of organizational cultures and the clash between the different varieties. But the book began very differently, with Handy hoping to find "laws governing the behavior of people and of organizations as sure and as immutable as the laws of physical sciences." He discovered, to his initial "dismay and disillusionment," that his subject had nothing to do with predictive certainty.

Too many variables, he discovered, hinge on any one organizational situation. And then there is "the inherent ability of the human being to override many of the influences on his behavior." Understanding organizations is still feasible, though, because:

- Most of the variables remain constant most of the time.
- Most individuals do not override the influencing factors most of the time.
- Most interpretations will be valid for the future as well as the past.
- Prediction tends to improve as the study turns from individuals to collections of individuals.

In the book, Handy describes no less than seven main schools of organizational thought, starting with "scientific management," fathered by the Quaker engineer Frederick Winslow Taylor (1856–1915). Then there was the school that looked at organizations in terms of human relations, and five others that concentrated respectively on bureaucracy, power, technology, systems, and institutions. None of them "proved to be wholly wrong" in their thinking, but none proved to be wholly right, either. So Handy set out to compile a "sort of personal anthology," which he intended to be of practical use to practicing managers.

Frederick Taylor

Taylor was the inspiration behind the 1880s' school of "scientific management." Radical for the time, it prescribed how businesses should be run, and advocated such procedures as planning ahead.

Looking at motivation

Achieving such a practical anthology was harder than it sounds. For instance, when Handy starts off looking at motivation, the book becomes rather dense without meeting Handy's hope "that motivation theories would reveal to me the true purpose of my life and my *raison d'être*." Instead, the theorists treated man as a semi-conscious mechanism, responding to a variety of impulses in a partly predictable way. The description, Handy admitted, was apt for many of his colleagues at work, but as for himself: "This wasn't me, I cried."

Motivation, true, was useful in understanding "how most individuals behaved, *given who they were*" [his italics]. But how does that "who" get created? Handy came to the conclusion that no single factor will do as an answer. Several factors are involved:

- The self-concept of the individual
- One's role in the organization
- The psychological contract between the individual and others in the organization
- One's perceptions of the situation

Handy found this motivational analysis inadequate. Unimpressed, he concluded: "We need to go much further to understand the behavior of people in organizations." But looking at the roles that people played inside organizations, and the interaction between those roles, proved a more fertile field. As he moves meticulously through the literature dealing with this subject, Handy shows how role problems, such as ambiguity, conflict, overload, and underload, produce individual tension, low morale, and poor communications.

Role stress is inherent in organizations, and can be either unhealthy or healthy. Role theory, Handy felt, provides one way of looking at stress, at individuals under stress, and at the situations that cause it. He suggested four remedies:

- Compartmentalize roles appropriately, particularly between work and family (that is, do not involve the wife in her husband's work, or, presumably, vice versa).
- Prepare for role transition (pay more attention to ways of learning a new role).
- Encourage a second career as a way out of the role underload of the sideways-shunted executive.
- Remember that many of the problems that exist in organizations have arisen from role strain, misconceptions about role, role underload, or bad communications because of false role expectations.

The leading role

Presumably the least underloaded and the most important of all the roles is "leader." In Handy's later work, leadership achieves (properly enough) a leading role in both senses. But, in the 1970s, he was ambivalent: "Leadership as a topic has rather a dated air about it." Two decades later, the topic is right back in fashion, but thinkers are no nearer to a satisfactory definition than Handy was in *Understanding Organizations*. There he wrote that "the role of a leader is a complex one, riddled with ambiguity, incompatibility, and conflict."

That sounds most unpromising. Handy devoted a section to the requirements of leadership, but its content is a good deal less than dynamic: for example, the leader should "be prepared to set moderately high standards for himself and his coworkers and to give and receive feedback on performance." Following on from that lame thought, Handy came perilously near to concluding that leadership was for all intents and purposes innate and unteachable, although the "individual and the organization can... build on what is already there."

This is plainly true of all human development, not just leadership. His tentative approach to this issue meant that Handy did not discuss to any great extent the role, often crucial, of the dominant individual in exercising power and influence. Charisma, he thought, resides not so much in the person as in the position. Handy saw that power, too, rested with position, and thus, to an extent, swung the balance of influence toward authoritarianism.

"Participative management," he observed, "implies expert power sources, influence by persuasion, and response by internalization. Great if it works." But generally it did not work: the likelihood of it happening amid "the hustle and bustle of organizational life" was low. Giving more control to subordinates, moreover, was a source of power that was "not obviously compatible with the emerging forms of the giant corporation, [nor] with the task requirements of most managerial roles in the organizations of today, or of tomorrow."

In view of Handy's later writing, that "or of tomorrow" seems inordinately pessimistic. He was at least equally unhappy about the prospects for management groups. With these, all too many things can go all too wrong:

- The task is inappropriate.
- The constraints are impossible.
- The group is badly led.
- It has inefficient procedures.

- It has the wrong people.
- It has too many people.
- It has too little power.
- It meets too infrequently.

If any one part is badly out of line, Handy concludes, the result will be either "an activation of negative power or a badly attended, noneffective group, wasting people, time, and space." Worse, "the chances of this happening are, in fact, very high. If 50 percent of managerial time is spent in groups, the cost of wasted time begins to look colossal, let alone the damage done by the use of negative power."

In the light of the latter, and still current, enthusiasm for group working, which Handy shares, this passage reads rather oddly. But Handy's pessimistic view of how organizations actually worked had not yet been succeeded by greater optimism about how they *might* work. Handy began to cross this line when he turned to the question of company culture. He concluded that the cultures of organizations rightly differ from each other, and that they are affected by a variety of factors, which in turn affect the diversity of structures and systems.

He argues that many organizational ills stem from the mismatches that exist between structures and cultures. This insight led Handy, more than in any other section of *Understanding Organizations*, to become what he termed "prescriptive." He tackled two crucial issues, those of differentiation and integration. Each organization needs to contain different cultures to cope with different types of activity: steady state (routine), innovation, crisis (the unexpected), and policy. "One culture," said Handy, "should not be allowed to swamp the organization." But the cultures have to work together.

Four types of culture

Handy concludes that for differentiation to succeed "there must be integration." He sets out seven "integrative devices," ranging from direct managerial supervision to "clustering" all the differences into one unit. But these issues proved less important in Handy's thought than he believed them to be at the time. In moving on, and moving far, his later books picked up on other themes, some of which had appeared almost incidentally in *Understanding Organizations*. One short section above all proved especially pregnant. It covers less than a dozen pages, the most original in the whole, long book, and defines four different types of organizational culture:

- The power culture
- The role culture
- The task culture
- The individual culture

The power culture "is frequently found in small entrepreneurial organizations, traditionally in the robber-baron companies of 19th-century America, occasionally in today's trade unions, and in some property, trading, and finance companies." The culture usually revolves around one dominant person.

The role culture is often stereotyped as bureaucracy. The structure for such a culture can be pictured as a Greek temple, with the pillars of the temple representing its functions or specialities. These pillars, which are strong in their own right, are the finance department, the purchasing department, the production facility, and so on. Their work, and the interaction between each of the pillars, is controlled by the following devices:

- Procedures for roles, such as job descriptions and authority definitions
- Procedures for communications, such as required sets of copies of memoranda
- Rules for settlement of disputes

As for the task culture, it could be seen not as a temple but as a net. The whole emphasis of this culture rests on getting the job done. It "seeks to bring together the appropriate resources, the right people at the right level of the organization, and to let them get on with it." The chosen members of the task force may include individuals who come from the fourth culture, that of idiosyncratic individualists. If there is a separate structure or organization for this last group, Handy noted, it can "exist only to serve and assist the individuals within it."

With these four cultures, Handy had found the germs of his first, great, original theme. Fully developed, it asserts that the cultures of organizations are crucial to their performance and that the dominant culture of traditional organizations is in the process of changing radically, not before time, in the face of irresistible pressures. By "culture," Handy meant that, like tribes and families, organizations have "their own ways of doing things, things that work for them and things that don't work."

Handy described four basic cultural patterns in these ways of working, and tentatively identified them with the Greek gods: Zeus (power), Apollo (role), Athena (task), and Dionysus (individual). For his next book, published in 1978, this metaphor took center stage and provided the title *Gods of Management*. Like his later, equally whimsical and obscure titles, this one had a strong point. In fact, the meaning is fundamental.

After completing *Understanding Organizations*, Handy became convinced that such understanding was impossible without the full comprehension of these four differing cultures. Moreover, culture was not the product of deliberate "scientific" management. Rather, organizational management was "more of a creative and political process, owing much to the prevailing culture and tradition in that place at that time." Enter the gods.

The dominance of Apollo

In *Gods of Management*, Handy expanded his definitions of four basic cultural patterns. An organization that follows Zeus, the all-powerful, capricious father of the gods, has a power culture and, accordingly, has its own father figure, the leader from whom all authority flows.

The culture is very different from that of Apollo, the god of reason, "for this culture works by logic and by rationality." The Apollonians, bowing to the deity of order, roles, and rules, vest authority in the system. Handy saw that their model – the role culture – had come to dominate nearly all the world's large organizations.

Athena, the warrior goddess, is best suited to preside over the task role. The people inside Athena's organizations, built around tasks, rather than roles, are problem solvers. They come together for a specific task, make up the rules as they go along, and disperse, proceeding to the next problem when the task is either completed or abandoned.

So far so good. It is easy to identify Handy's account of the gods with actual organizations: a multinational oil giant like Shell (Handy's former employer) with Apollo; any number of firms dominated by founding entrepreneurs with Zeus; advertising agencies with Athena.

Dionysus, "the god of the self-oriented individual, the first existentialist" is a more difficult case. His specialities – wine and song – at first sight have little to do with any organizations, except for cabarets, which are often, as it happens, in the thrall of a Zeus. Handy recognized this difficulty; in a book about organizations, he had identified a form of organizational culture that did not exist and could not exist, at least not in the same way as the others.

Zeus, Apollo, and Athena, in their very different styles, preside over organizations that in turn preside over their members. In Handy's Dionysian vision, the organization is dominated by individuals who are members only because they choose to be. This culture, Handy observes, "is something which causes shudders in any more usual organization or managers – precisely because of the lack of mandated control." However, managers will seldom need to shudder. Where will they ever meet Dionysus?:

> "One would not expect to find many such organizations around, certainly not in the business or industrial scene, where organizations, by their charters, have objectives that outlive and outgrow their employees."

The inclusion of the Dionysian nonorganization is, however, of vital importance to Handy's theory of organizations, which he calls "a Theory of Cultural

"The best way to run an efficient chocolate factory will not be the right way to run an architects' partnership, a primary school, or a construction site. Different cultures, and gods, are needed for different tasks."
Gods of Management

Propriety." This holds that what matters is getting the right culture in the right place for the right purpose, which all sounds quite bland and neutral; Handy even calls it a "low definition" theory, which "suggests rather then prescribes." In fact, Handy proceeded to develop the four gods idea toward a distinctly prescriptive end. The predominant form of organization, he plainly feels, is producing the wrong culture in the wrong place for the wrong purpose.

Organizations can only be righted, Handy argues, by admitting the cult of Dionysus into their office blocks and other places of work – like it or not. Handy is explicit about the topsy-turvy consequences. In "this fourth existential culture, the organization exists to help the individual achieve his purpose," not, as in the usual dispensation, the other way around. Handy is not thinking just of the need to allow a relatively few talented individuals their freedom: "the cult of Dionysus is growing and is no longer related to individual talent."

In some way, management needs to create a contradiction in terms: a Dionysian establishment, a disorganized organization. Handy is careful to avoid identifying himself as a prophet of this vision, but *Gods of Management* really does plead a cause. Like Luther railing at the Roman Catholic Church, Handy is protesting against what he sees as the mounting failure of the traditional organization:

> "... the chosen route to efficiency via concentration and specialization which resulted in the multilayered and multistructured organization has reached a dead end."

"No culture, or mix of cultures, is bad or wrong in itself, only inappropriate to its circumstances." *Gods of Management*

Diseconomies of scale

One of Handy's explanations for the failure of the traditional organization is familiar: scale means largeness, and "scale creates costs as well as economies," although, in normal circumstances, the economies outweigh the costs. Large organizations, as everybody knows, are less flexible, which offsets the strengths of their wider scope, although by no means entirely. But Handy does not rely on organizational economics to make his case against bigness: "more importantly, it runs counter to the cultural preferences of most of the people it needs to make it work."

What were these truly widespread ("most of the people") cultural longings? Handy was apparently contending that "most" people are Athenians or Dionysians by preference, yet he writes: "An Apollonian structure staffed by Athenians and Dionysians would be an expensive disaster." Whether or not that is true, the argument hinges on Handy's unsupported and unprovable view of human preferences. Those preferences explain why, in his calm but almost apocalyptic prophecy, "the chosen responses of most organizations are not going to work because they all seek to find ways of perpetuating the Apollonian dominance."

Do most people truly prefer either to work in dedicated, fluid groups, or as footloose, self-motivating individuals? Handy is here articulating the familiar refusal of the intellectual, whose work is almost always Athenian or Dionysian, to believe that mass-production workers, clerks, shop assistants, even middle managers, can enjoy their work. As thinking has become more important in relation to doing – brains conquering brawn – this intellectual revulsion has acquired greater relevance. But rules, roles, and order – the Apollonian characteristics – are by no means inimical to the human spirit or to human progress.

Changing work patterns

However, that does not stop Handy from arguing that Apollo's day is done, and adding a polite good riddance. His chapters "suggest," or rather forecast, that "the employment organization, centered around the works or the office," will give way to "a more contractual, dispersed, and federal organization." The potential consequences are greatly to Handy's liking:

- More small businesses, particularly in services
- More part-time work in all institutions
- More opportunity for more people to combine jobs with other interests in life
- More work located near to where people live

Handy thought that communities would perhaps become more complete when they ceased to be mere dormitories. Flexible working lives, built around several jobs rather than one, might become the norm rather than the exception. In other words, everybody's life in the future could be like Handy's own in the present. He might think that desirable, but the possible alternative is not. Handy feared that the old split between labor and owners or management might be replaced by a new split between "professionals and key staff, with job security and fringe benefits, and the secondary fringe of temporary labor, part-time help, and self-employment – free maybe, but often poor."

All of the above cautious predictions, the welcome and the unwelcome, have come to pass in varying degrees. But the hard fact remains that the world and national economies remain dominated by very large, structured organizations of the type Handy condemns to slow death. Many of these organizations have grown vastly larger (in everything except numbers employed). Unlike the dinosaurs, they have adapted to changing conditions. But Handy gives no timescale for their disappearance. What he does is make a full and fair case for abandoning Apollo, which was to be the next stage of his great theme.

Ideas into action

- Organize your business to fit its real-life circumstances, not some ideal model.
- Remember that many organizational problems stem from people's difficulties with their roles.
- Make sure you get the right culture in the right place for the right purpose.
- Do not let the "Apollonians," with their specified rules and roles, dominate the organization.
- Rely increasingly on "Athenians," task-force members who tackle specific projects.
- Make room for the "Dionysians," talented individuals who "do their own thing."
- Provide more opportunities for people to work part-time and near to their homes.

2

Balancing the organization

The growth of Dionysian individualism in organizations • How and when people revert to their favorite culture • **The three critical areas of management – thinking and learning, influencing and changing, motivating and rewarding** • Letting each part of the organization develop its own methods of coordination and control • **The waning of the employment society** • The danger of sabotage by the "organizational hijack" • **Why megacorporations are unmanageable and have to change**

The plural title of Handy's second book, *Gods of Management*, is slightly misleading; a single god of management would have given a sharper picture. Zeus organizations rise and fall with the founder/father's physical life cycle, and have to become more Apollonian to survive. Purely Athenian organizations are few and far between (and task forces can work perfectly well inside large, bureaucratic organizations, anyway). Dionysian organizations (or dis-organizations) can hardly be found anywhere. Apollo is the true god of management.

Handy's account of the supergod's creations is full of insight and deep understanding. His criticism, however, is heavily influenced by his experience of what he believes to be a Dionysian culture: the university. Its professionals possess several advantages over managers:

- Job security
- Agreed pay scales
- "Allocated territories or spheres of influence"
- Guarantees of independence
- Selection or promotion (usually) by groups of equals
- Uninterrupted power in their particular workplace
- Freedom from normal industrial disciplines

Dismissal, money, perks, and punishment are not in the hands of the academics' nominal leader, either. In this environment, command can operate only by consent, and not by delegated authority. This culture, says Handy, "causes shudders" in any more usual organization or manager "precisely because of the lack of mandated control." Here, however, he surely exaggerates both the freedom enjoyed by academics and the authoritarian power of business managers.

Large sets of jobs

Academics are subject to (and generally resent) all manner of constraints, while managers ultimately cannot manage effectively without the consent of the managed. The degree of freedom, of managers or managed, depends on highly variable circumstances and relationships. By Handy's own admission, his Greek gods never reign entirely alone. He asks: "Why would these three very different gods be required in the same organization?," and answers that organizations "are just large sets of jobs to be done." He divides these tasks into three types: steady state, development, and "asterisk."

The first type of task is programmable and predictable, and ideal for systems, routines, rules, and procedures. This is Apollo country and may represent 80 percent of all work. The second type requires the development of solutions to situations or problems: enter Athena and the Athenians. The third type, the "asterisk," is the realm of "personal intervention" and thus of both Zeus and Dionysus. Asterisks are "the exceptions, the occasions where the rulebook has failed, the emergencies where instinct, and speed, are likely to be better than logical analysis or creative problem-solving." Handy's prognosis is puzzling. Why cannot "creative problem-solving" be accomplished instinctively and fast? His conclusion is equally problematic:

> "Management happens when these activities are linked together in an appropriate fashion and given some common purpose or direction… The manager therefore has to embrace within himself all four cultures."

If that is the case, the separate significance of the cultures becomes unclear. If organizations have to possess all four cultures (otherwise they have no "management"), the four gods metaphor comes under strain. Handy meets this difficulty by saying that "the simultaneous call of four gods is too much for most people." So they revert to their favorite culture, "particularly when tired or stressed" (which seems a strange qualification). Thus, instead of organizations constraining the natural instincts of the people within – the generally accepted view – it is the people who constrain the organization.

In addition, Handy states that while organizations need more than one god, individuals are monotheists. To each his own god, which means his own different approach to the three "critical areas" of management:

- Thinking and learning
- Influencing and changing
- Motivating and rewarding

The individual preferences, Handy suggests, explain why organizations are the way they are. So, if Apollo dominates most organizations, it follows that their inhabitants must be predominantly Apollonians – not by force, but by nature. This is a contradiction that he never resolves.

Left-brained Apollonians

Apollonians are left-brain thinkers: logical, sequential, and analytical. They learn by acquiring more knowledge and skills through training, and they influence by exercising the authority that has been granted to them by the system. In this culture, change can come about only by altering roles and responsibilities, or changing the whole network of rules and procedures.

When it comes to motivation and reward, Apollonians are, once again, organization people to the core. They want the security of long-term organized employment, fringe benefits – especially pensions – and status. Handy does not actually mention graduated pay scales and bonuses, but these are presumably part of the picture, too. Plainly, such preferences determine a whole set of approved behaviors – ones that members of Handy's two other predominant organizational cultures find objectionable. Thus, "a Zeus will chafe under an Apollonian regime and forget to trust his intuition or his network." Then, "Apollonians will be seen as useful but boring" by Athenians. The Dionysians live, of course, on a different planet: "They like to be individuals, exceptions to all generalizations," but presumably not to this generalization itself.

In fact, Handy admits that it is difficult, and perhaps even mistaken, to describe Dionysus as a class at all. But he also points out that: "… the growth of individualism in organizations is becoming one of the central dilemmas of society… so the difficult must be attempted." This attempt is essential to support Handy's central idea, that "the healthy, happy organization is one that uses the appropriate methods and assumptions of influence in a particular culture." For the purposes of Handy's argument, that must certainly include Dionysians.

"Differences are necessary and good for organizational health. Monotheism, the pursuit of a single god, must be wrong for most organizations. But the choice and blend of gods cannot be haphazard. The wrong god in the wrong place means pain and inefficiency."
Gods of Management

Cultural coexistence

In this theory, the four cultures can coexist, and must, to create a wholly successful organization. In practice, the conflicts are deep-seated, and the dominant culture will use its dominance to resolve the issue to suit itself. Apollonian techniques and rules, writes Handy, "get ignored by Zeus figures unless it suits their proposers to use them." That is only one example of what happens if the mix of culture is "wrong, or badly balanced, or is not changed when change is needed." The result is "slack" or ineffectiveness – "the lurking cancer of organizations."

The chances of avoiding, or curing, the cancer by reaching an effective mix will be influenced by the size, life cycles, work patterns, and people in the organization. The larger the company, the more Apollo thrives. "The higher the rate of change, the larger the influence of Athena." The more that work flows and needs to be replicated, the stronger the Apollonian influence again. Handy's generalizations, however, need a great deal of qualification. People, he confesses, do not fit neatly into the above plan: "The tendencies of the 'people forces' are too varied to be summarized."

Whatever balance is achieved, anyway, will not last. "Organizations must respond continually to the environment" and their circumstances. Here, Handy cites the familiar cycle of growth. Once a business reaches a certain size, its founder (Zeus) must bring in professional managers (Apollonians). Then Athenians are required to develop the business further. So "management," as noted earlier, comes to mean the coordination of all three, and sometimes four, gods in one whole.

If there is "a mismatch between the demands of the work and the ways of managing it, success has bred inefficiency through cultural imbalance." The obvious answer is to change the balance. The catch is that "cultural change of the order needed in these situations is hard to bring about deliberately." Handy notes that organizations usually need to be frightened into major change by "imminent bankruptcy, a slump in sales, major strikes," and so on. Then new people, new directions, and new groupings alter the corporate constellation.

For that to be effective, "linkage between the cultures is essential," involving cultural tolerance, bridges, and a common language. If these fail, mixed-up management, and thus Handy's dreaded "slack," will occur. But, sadly, the different gods have different ways of coordination:

> "The first step, then, to effective linkage is to allow each part of the organization to develop its own appropriate methods of coordination and control and to tolerate differences between the cultures. Otherwise, one enters the 'spiral of distrust,' when what seems sensible coordination to you appears intrusive control to the other."

Building bridges

Handy stresses that cultural tolerance is not enough. The bridges that are also required take various forms. The first question is: "How many bridges and where?," to which Handy answers, the fewer the better. The second question is the method of bridging. Do you proceed by grouping, that is "putting all the functions... into one group with one objective," central information, or liaison ("the most tenuous form of bridge")? Handy obviously regards bridging as a messy affair; and his own account is appropriately messy itself. He finally boils it down to the swing of the pendulum between centralization and decentralization, and arrives at a gloomy conclusion:

"The search for balance is never-ending. The swinging is inevitable, but, if done with cultural understanding, the pain is less."

Handy is similarly doubtful about efforts to create a common language: "Language… can be a barrier as much as a bridge." He points out that the vocabulary of organizations includes buzzwords and statistics, and that this vocabulary governs how people act: "The choice of what you count, what you compare with what, what you show to whom, has a clear effect on behavior." A Zeus culture's internal memo "will often read like a family letter"; Apollonian memos, however, bristle with initials. All these codes, writes Handy, are baffling to the outsider and may even be misunderstood inside the organization.

In sum, efforts to resolve the clash of cultures cannot rescue Apollo from a crucial dilemma. "The pressures to become more Apollonian, to make organizations tidier and more formal, are pressing and convincing, but so are the opposing pressures to recognize the individuals who make up these organizations and the need to give them more scope, more rights, and more independence."

According to Handy, these more individualistic pressures are inexorable outcomes of a richer and freer society. The end result will be "new kinds of organizations, new structures, and new ways of relating individuals to organizations" – in short, "an organizational revolution" that will affect not only the way that institutions are managed, but also the way in which people plan and live their lives. The prophet even dated his prophecy, suggesting that "the year 2000 will see the waning of the employment society as we have known it."

The root cause of this is the Apollonian paradox, which embodies "the tendency for Apollo to self-destruct. For just as size creates an internal need for Apollonian methods, so the very increase in that culture tends to make the total organization less responsive to its environment, less capable of changing, more dinosaurlike than ever – impressive but out of touch, and often out of control."

The symptoms of Apollonian breakdown are familiar, such as unfinished tasks, or nobody knowing how or by whom decisions are made. These organizations can be seen as "inevitably alienating places," which cannot tolerate much discretion, because it would violate their consistency.

> "One can redesign jobs to allow marginally greater discretion, introduce flexitime or autonomous groups, create work councils, but these all remain placebos…, to relieve the pain and alleviate the inherent incompatibility between man and this kind of work."

In Apollonian organizations, the individual is a *role* more than a *person*; initiative comes from above, not from within; and creativity is too often counted as disruption. This flies in the face not only of creativity but also of social and educational changes. "We are bringing up the young in a Dionysian tradition – individuality and personal expression – with Athenian overtones – groups, projects, and shared values. It is not surprising that they then reject the Apollonian culture when they begin to meet it at work."

Organizational hijack

This growing clash in Western society between organizational logic and the feelings of the individual leads to what Handy calls "the organizational hijack." This occurs when a "cog, or work group, a subassembly unit, a department" brings the overtightly designed organization to a halt by withholding labor, skill, or talent. Handy for some reason bleakly exaggerates this negative power:

"The monolithic overtight design of our organizations is an invitation to hijack and a major contributory cause to wage inflation. We have given what is called *negative power* in huge amounts to those people most likely to use it. Apollonian cultures come equipped with this time bomb, which will destroy the whole temple if it is not defused."

The megacorporations, Handy firmly concludes, have reached a crossroads. "The truth is that they have become, literally, unmanageable." He sees great consequences following as organizations structure and rebalance in the sheer need to stay alive:

"In 30 years' time, it may be as odd to talk of an employee as it already is to talk of servants." The new technologies need Dionysians and Athenians before Apollonians, and that means looser organizations whose key workers earn fees rather than wages. Even for the professional core, "employment will be only a phase of life," not much longer than the educational phase. Early retirement will become the norm for expensive top managers and specialists.

The displaced middle-aged will at best enter a world of small-time employment, of small Zeus figures, private Dionysians, and illicit (black market) Athenians. "Whether we like it or not, more and more of us are going to have to follow Zeus and Dionysus for more and more of our lives." Tightly regulated but loosely structured, the remaining organizations will be smaller and less dominating, "with less room in them and more selection about both entry and exit. Even the people in these smaller temples may no longer think of themselves as employees."

Sharing ownership

Handy argues that sheer size, and the consequences of it – complexity, inflexibility, and slack – are not the only causes of the flight from Apollo; another is the "reluctance to be owned by another, even if the pay is good." More and more requests for a share in the fruits of ownership will follow, notably through stock options. "It is an obvious way in which to marry labor and capital, with the result that top managers do not, in those firms, usually think of themselves as employees but as co-owners, partners, or as members of the organization."

Much of the above is highly debatable, including the last statement. Handy also foresaw a spread of ownership lower down the organization, and more cooperatives. The first has come to pass, thanks more to politicians than to internal pressures in corporations. The second has not happened. Nor has employee ownership (any more than employee representation, Euro-style) had much impact on the realities of management.

Handy concluded that if Dionysians could not get more ownership to replace their dependence on the Apollonian structure, "then the right to be consulted, personally, will become more pressing; in other words, organizations will have to get smaller until the individual, not his or her representative, can be heard at the top." Handy's thinking here is certainly wishful, as organizations have, in fact, been getting much larger, mostly through merger and acquisition, and through globalization.

His forecast that women will have a "proper influence" on organizations as these become more Athenian or Dionysian may also be a little wishful. Women will, true, fit easily into a more flexible world, in which credentials matter most, in which fewer people can define themselves, Apollo-style, as an ICI man or a Shell woman. Many people will have "flexilives," with multiple-job portfolios of work, as opposed to a single occupation; this, too, will suit many women well.

Problems of change

Flexilives also greatly suit Handy's philosophy. But he foresaw problems. What would people live on? How would they educate themselves? And how would they protect themselves? "Put rather starkly," Handy writes, "if we are working half the hours we used to and if we can look forward to twice as many years after employment, we ought to be putting aside, as a nation or as individuals, four times as much money for our retirement." But nothing like that is happening.

As for education, organizations now need to think of themselves as schools, encouraging their people to acquire the means of freedom, even if "they sometimes set themselves free before the organization would have wanted it." Protection for all will have to come from broader-based unions, otherwise, the latter will effectively signal their own decline. (Unions have indeed declined, but not for the reason Handy gives.)

Handy's predictions are a mixed bunch, both in their depth and in their accuracy. Their general thrust has certainly proved correct. But it is impossible to avoid the evidence of wishful thinking. Looking into his crystal ball, Handy too often saw what he wanted to happen, rather than what was truly likely to come about. In particular, organizations have proved much more resilient than he expected. He saw, it is true, one escape route, one way in which firms could cheat fate:

"Unusually, however, and fortunately, their destiny is in their own hands. Organizations may usually wither and decay instead of changing, but it does not have to be that way. This book is written in the hope that if more managers understand what is happening and what possibilities are open to them, then more will experiment with the future, instead of ignoring it."

The level of corporate experimentation, right into the 21st century, has remained low, however. Handy could be right in arguing that "our society may well decay as its organizations wither." But the day of withering seems to have been indefinitely postponed.

Ideas into action

- Adopt the academic work-style, where command operates only by consent.
- Prepare for the exceptions and emergencies where the rulebook will fail you.
- Combine the four basic types of culture to obtain lasting success.
- Continually review the organization and adjust it to the changing environment.
- Give individuals as much scope, as many rights, and as much independence as you can.
- Keep the organizational design flexible and loose to reduce vulnerability.
- Spread the fruits of ownership as widely in the organization as possible.

Organizing the culture

The culture of an organization – the way it works and what people believe about it – has a major effect on performance and overall results. Identify the dominant culture of your organization using the Handy-based questionnaires set out in this masterclass. Then seek to balance the cultural mix to obtain maximum effectiveness from everyone.

Understanding the cultures

Handy identified four cultural patterns, each characterized by a different Greek god. Most organizations are dominated by one of the three cultural patterns below. The fourth culture, ruled by Dionysus, is that of the individual, and its followers are not interested in organization or in organized cultures.

The Three Types of Organizational Culture		
1 Power ruled by Zeus	**2 Role** ruled by Apollo	**3 Task** ruled by Athena

Each Handy culture has its particular strengths. The personal power of Zeus dominance can work wonderfully well even in large companies – given the right father figure. But larger companies also require the order and control that Apollo's role culture embodies, with its emphasis on systems, routines, and predictability. In today's fast-moving environment both Zeus and Apollo find the Athenian task-oriented approach increasingly essential.

Finding the right balance

Achieving the right balance between Handy's gods involves countering the excesses that all three cultures can easily develop – respectively, autocracy, bureaucracy, and disintegration. A successful mix will also embrace individualistic Dionysus.

The combination of all four gods satisfies Handy's definition of good management. For this you must use Zeus to provide purpose and direction, Apollo to look after the steady-state needs, Athena to keep the organization moving forward, and Dionysus to supply the vital spark of creativity.

1 Identifying power

Handy compares the Zeus culture to a spider's web. All authority radiates outward from the center, and the closer managers are to that center, the more important they are.

Following Zeus

To discover if your organization is ruled by Zeus, answer Yes or No to the following propositions. Do they describe the organization's typical values, beliefs, and forms of behavior?

- A good boss is strong, decisive, firm but fair.
- A good subordinate is hardworking, loyal, resourceful, and trustworthy.
- A good member gives first priority to the personal demands of the boss.
- People who do well here are politically aware risk-takers.
- The organization treats individuals as people at the disposal of the bosses.
- People are controlled and influenced by rewards, punishments, or charisma.
- It is legitimate to control others if you have more power.
- Tasks are assigned here on the personal say-so of the bosses.
- Competition is for personal power and advantage.

Analysis

- Nine "Yes" answers: a pure power culture, dominated by a Zeus figure or figures.
- Nine "Nos": the culture is remarkably free of bossism.
- Three or fewer "Yes" answers: the culture is not generally autocratic.
- Three or fewer "Nos": the culture is generally autocratic.

Countering autocracy

If your organization is dominated by the power culture it will need to resist autocracy. To do this, increase the number of Athenalike autonomous task forces. Task forces are mini-Zeus cultures, with a boss, a web, and a mission. Autocrats can understand their value and the way they work, and can therefore accept them in the organization. Such groups do not threaten the autocrat's power, but they do make it less easy for him or her to exert centralized control.

2 Defining the roles

Handy represents the highly organized, systematic Apollonian role culture as a Greek temple with each pillar representing a function or division, and control resting with the senior executives at the top. Is this your organizational picture?

Organization man

To discover if your organization is ruled by Apollo, answer Yes or No to the following set of propositions. Are they or are they not the organization's typical values, beliefs, and forms of behavior?

- A good boss is impersonal and correct.
- A good subordinate is responsible and reliable.
- A good member gives first priority to duties, responsibilities, and customary standards.
- People who do well here are conscientious, responsible, and loyal.
- The organization treats individuals as if they are under contract.
- People are controlled and influenced impersonally by enforcing procedures and standards.
- It is legitimate to control others if you have formal responsibility.
- Tasks are assigned here on functions and responsibility.
- Competition is for high formal status.

Analysis

- Nine "Yes" answers: a classic "organization man" culture, dominated by Apollo and the Apollonians.
- Nine "Nos": the culture is remarkably free from systems and controls.
- Three or fewer "Yes" answers: the culture is not generally bureaucratic.
- Three or fewer "Nos": a definite inclination toward bureaucracy.

Countering the excesses

The potential excesses of an Apollonian role culture are dehumanized behaviors and the creation of a powerful bureaucracy. Countering these excesses requires finding ways of injecting individualism into what is essentially a collective culture.

One way of forcing a general cultural change is to alter the reward system. Apollonians love rigid pay scales tied to rigid hierarchies, under peculiar rules, such as "nobody can be promoted more than two grades at a time" or "lower grades cannot be placed over higher grades." Do not reward people simply for coming to work. Give exceptional rewards for exceptional performance, and make the rewards psychic (celebrations, congratulations, etc.) as well as real (money and promotion).

Another way of reducing the impersonal nature of the role culture, in which people are treated not as human beings but as cogs in a well-oiled machine, is to apply the Golden Rule: "Do unto others as you would have them do unto you." Until a Golden Rule culture is established, dehumanized behavior will be the norm.

Changing specific behaviors

You can change the culture of an organization only by changing the behavior of its individual members. There are eight specific Apollonian behaviors that together lead to a dehumanized and bureaucratic organization. Each one has an antidote, which, if routinely employed, will decrease these unhelpful tendencies.

Ways to Change Apollonian Behaviors

Bad behavior	Antidote
1 Refusing to entertain contradictory/unorthodox views.	Empower people to oppose the consensus.
2 Ignoring evidence that argues against chosen policies.	Require proposers to provide a full list of pros and cons.
3 Making decisions that are unethical or inhumane.	Publish a code of ethics and appoint an ombudsman.
4 Seeing opponents and colleagues as stereotypes rather than individuals.	Arrange face-to-face meetings supervised by an impartial facilitator.
5 Pressuring people to conform to group opinions.	Reward individual initiatives and demand new ideas.
6 Forming cliques that keep to themselves.	Send outsiders into groups as co-opted members.
7 Leaving people in groups no option but unanimity.	Solicit everybody's opinion in rotation.
8 Continuing with policies that have been proved false.	Make admitting and correcting mistakes imperative.

3 Tackling the tasks

More and more managers are working in temporary groups that cut across departmental boundaries, mingle disciplines, and exist to complete a common task. The Athenian task-force mode is changing most Apollonian cultures. How far has it affected your culture?

The task-force mode

To discover how much influence Athena exerts in your organization, answer Yes or No to the following propositions. Are they or are they not the organization's typical values, beliefs, and forms of behavior?

- A good boss is egalitarian and can be influenced.
- A good subordinate is self-motivated and open to ideas.
- A good member gives first priority to the requirements of the task.
- People who do well here are technically competent, effective, and committed.
- The organization treats individuals as committed coworkers.
- People are controlled and influenced by personal commitment to achieving goals.
- It is legitimate to control others if you know more about the task.
- Tasks are assigned here on ability to execute.
- Competition is for excellence of contribution.

Analysis

- Nine "Yes" answers: an organization that puts performance ahead of personalities and gives people many opportunities to succeed.
- Nine "Nos": the culture is either authoritarian or bureaucratic, or both.
- Three or fewer "Yes" answers: the culture is not an open one.
- Three or fewer Nos: the culture is open – most of the time.

Improving the network

The task-oriented culture is essentially a network. It may well extend outside the borders of the company to suppliers and customers. To optimize the effectiveness of this kind of culture and to ensure its continued dominance in your organization, use the latest information technology to connect yourself to the network, and think of yourself as an essential node.

4 Injecting creativity

Any culture, despite its defects, can succeed with just one great idea – one so powerful that it transcends those defects. Creative self-oriented Dionysian individuals can provide such ideas. Does your organization contain enough of these people?

Creative Dionysus

Dionysus has nothing to do with organization, but he has a lot to do with culture. God of the nonorganization, his disciples are primarily individual and creative thinkers who find it very difficult to work in large, highly structured, Apollo-ruled organizations.

No organization can do without this type, however, if it is to deal successfully with the exceptional situations where the normal responses have failed to provide a result. In these circumstances only the quick, individualistic thinking of Dionysian types is likely to provide a solution. Are you such a Dionysian individual? Do you:

- Give your subordinates stimulating work?
- Respect the needs and values of others?
- Give priority to individuals and their needs?
- Excel in personal relationships?
- Treat colleagues as interesting and valuable people?
- Get deeply interested in and excited by your work?
- Manage with the full consent of others?
- Make all appointments strictly on merit?
- Compete primarily to beat your own best standards?

Working within an organization

The attributes and behaviors of a Dionysian individual would be applauded by all of Handy's three organizational cultures: the autocrat, the bureaucrat, and the taskmaster would all say that they want managers to fit this excellent pattern.

But saying and doing are not the same thing. In organizations of every culture, you will find lip service to the Dionysian ideal, coupled with actions, procedures, and interactions that make Dionysian behavior difficult in practice. Do not despair. Bear in mind that, while cultures are collective, the collective is made up of individuals. Live up to your best Dionysian ideals at all times.

3

Working in the new society

The principles of "the Shamrock Organization" • Treating the three leaves of the shamrock in separate ways • **The evolving world of the flexible labor force** • Getting the core of the shamrock right, and managing it right • **The rise of the "federal" company and the role of its center** • How "subsidiarity" will become a self-fulfilling prophecy • **Using a fast-track Japanese approach to promoting young people** • The Triple I organization with intelligence, information, and ideas

Charles Handy began his questioning march into the future in his 1989 book, *The Age of Unreason*. Here, he unveiled "the Shamrock Organization," a new coinage that was his response to the changes in the world of work. These had been created by changes in organizations that were themselves adapting to that same changing world of work. He wastes no time on which came first here, the chicken or the egg, but leaps straight into the heart of the matter: the increased pressure for results.

The new thinking on organizations, Handy wrote, is visible in several ways, including a shake-up in the careers and lives of managers, and the emergence of the shamrock: "the new alliance of different types of work and workers."

The structure of the shamrock

Handy uses the Irish national emblem to symbolize this division of today's organizations into "three very different groups of people, groups with different expectations, managed differently, paid differently, organized differently":

1 The professional core of qualified professionals, technicans, and managers.
2 People outside the organization, but who work for it as subcontractors.
3 The flexible labor force of part-time workers and temporary workers.

Between them, the essential people in the core own the knowledge that distinguishes one organization from another. Organizations cannot afford to lose them, so go to great lengths to bind them with "hoops of gold, with high salaries, fringe benefits, and German cars." In return, the core members have to work hard and long, with total commitment and flexibility.

The huge expense of these people means that companies cut down on their numbers as much as possible. "Every successful organization," Handy says, "will tell you that they have at least quadrupled their turnover in the last 10 years, but have halved their professional core." Contracting out, of course, reduces the core need. Handy calls the work involved "nonessential," but he is wrong: some firms even contract out the assembly of their key products. But the principle is clear: work that could be done by others is given to specialists who can, in theory, do it better for less cost.

The third leaf, the flexible labor force, now the fastest growing part of the employment scene, has existed for a long time. So, in embryo, has the three-leaved workforce. "What is different today is the scale," writes Handy. "Each of the leaves is now significant."

Managing the leaves

Each leaf also demands separate treatment, starting with the professional core of key people, including managers. Their lives are going to resemble those of independent consultants, working in flat structures, rarely promoted, but often rewarded in ways other than salaries and benefits:

"Economic necessity... will force more organizations to rethink the way they reward their senior core people, turning them... into partners rather than employees, colleagues rather than bosses and subordinates, names not roles."

"The contractual fringe" has always earned its rewards differently, being paid for results, not time, and in fees, not wages. This "means that the central organization can exercise control only by specifying the results, not by overseeing the methods." Handy calls this revolutionary for managers who are used to the maxim: "Control the means and the methods, and the results will be as they should be." In fact, many outsourcing companies do oversee methods intently, and Handy underplays the crucial role of trust in these relationships. Nevertheless, he approves in general: "The contract [between "employer" and "worker"] is now more explicit and in many respects more healthy for that."

The more worrying leaf is the third, the flexible workers. "In crude terms, these people are the labor market... into which employers dip as they like, and when they need, for as little money as they have to pay." Handy condemns this as shortsighted philosophy and calls for changed attitudes:

> "If the flexible labor force is seen to be a valuable part of the organization [the latter] will be prepared to invest in them, to provide training, even training leading to qualifications, to give them some status and some privileges (including paid holidays and sick leave entitlement).... Then and only then will the organization get the temporary or part-time help that it needs to the standards it requires."

This is more pious hope than confident prediction. But Handy draws a clear picture of an evolving world in which customers do more and more work for their suppliers (making their own reservations over the internet, for example); in which more and more people are based at home, as networked employees or as "telecommuters"; in which more and more head offices, small and often half-empty, function as a "working club"; in which "homework," once just another means of exploiting female labor, may become an efficient and rewarding way of tapping the pool of educated women with small children.

In his last words on the shamrock, Handy says: "The core is the critical hub of an organizational network. It is essential to get it right and to manage it right." The network will have important features other than the three parts of the shamrock. Alongside the latter, Handy sees "the federal organization" developing. He means the alliance of a variety of individual groups under a common flag with some shared identity. It is the answer to the paradox that businesses need to be big and small simultaneously.

The federal organization

According to Handy, "big" provides marketplace and financial clout, and possibly economies of scale, while "small" gives flexibility, "as well as the sense of community for which individuals [and Handy] increasingly hanker." Federalism differs from decentralization, in which the center delegates, initiates, directs, and ultimately controls. Federalism features "reverse thrust organizations," in which "the initiative, the drive, and the energy come mostly from the parts, with the center an influencing force, relatively low in profile."

Handy sees the rise of federalism as another involuntary piece of discontinuity. Organizations have cut down their cores, and have fewer people to interpret the information transmitted by the new technology, who can then act on that information to control decentralized operations. The consequences for managements are inevitable:

> "It is better in the end that they do not even try, but concentrate instead on the things they can control and the decisions which they alone can take. Small cores make federalism ultimately inevitable, and large cores make decentralization ultimately too expensive."

What, then, does the federal center do? Handy says that it must be more than a banker. It must manage the future. It must "think in terms of global strategies which may link one or more of the autonomous parts." It must "cling to its key functions of [recruiting] new people and [finding] new money." But fuller control is not on the menu, even if control is reduced to making the long-term decisions and leaving implementation to the parts. That reduction still "reeks of the old engineering language of management." The new language requires a new image of the corporation.

The center is now genuinely the center, and not the top. It makes its decisions in consultation with the chiefs of the parts. "It has to be a place of persuasion, of argument leading to consensus." Leadership of ideas takes over from leadership by personality. The leadership may even be shared by two or three people, backed by "a staff whose concerns will largely be with the future, with plans and possibilities, scenarios, and options."

Independence and unity

Today, most large organizations reflect this new image, if only in part. Handy's comment remains true: "Because organizations evolve there are, as yet, few federal corporations in pure form." Perhaps that will always be true, given the difficulty of balancing independence with a meaningful unity. "Too much independence… can lead to breakaway or to a random collection of disparate parts." Misunderstood federalism becomes inefficient decentralization. True understanding, though, involves new concepts, like "subsidiarity."

By this Handy means giving away power: "the federal organization will not work unless those in the center not only *have* to let go of some of their power but actually *want* to do so." Only then will the new decision-makers be trusted to reach and implement the right decisions. Handy accepts that Catch-22 applies: you want to give responsibility only to people who are capable, but you do not know if they are capable until they have been given responsibility. To resolve the catch, Handy turns to hope. The best subsidiarity will attract the best people: so "ultimately subsidiarity is a self-fulfilling prophecy."

He puts forward as an alternative analogy the "inside-out doughnut" (see pp. 89–101). The job consists of a core, which is clearly defined, and a surrounding space where you have discretion. Federal organizations "require large doughnuts, whether they are group ones or individual ones." The organization has to be managed by specifying the results that are required from each doughnut. This is Management by Results – "a major change in our ways of managing," and one that requires "a new language to describe them."

Much of that language ("of federations and networks, of alliances and influences… shamrocks and doughnuts") has been popularized or invented by Handy. He thinks that it must be recognized as the *right* language. "No one, after all, has ever liked being managed, for anyone who has tried to run an organization has always known that it was more like running a small country than a machine." Handy has no room for so-called scientific management, saying that only theorists have tried to "apply the hard rules of number and logic and mechanics to an essentially soft system."

Anyone who tries to manage without those hard numbers, though, is certainly courting early and severe failure. The hard-soft conflict is another basic paradox of management, which Handy glosses over in his enthusiasm for the new language. As he notes, the shift away from hard concepts is general: "Leadership is now fashionable and the language of leadership increasingly important."

Principles for leaders

Handy believes that leadership has to be endemic in organizations, whose people, if they have pretensions to be anybody, "must begin to think and act like a leader." What does that mean? Handy recognizes that leadership is "mysterious" and hard to define, but settles for this statement: "A leader shapes and shares a vision which gives point to the work of others."

Creating and sharing a vision, however, is much easier said than done, as Handy recognizes. But he isolates five principles for leaders to live by:

1. The vision must be different: "A plan or a strategy which is a projection of the present or a replica of what everybody else is doing is not a vision."
2. The vision must make sense to others: "It must stretch people's imaginations but still be within the bounds of possibility." It must be related to people's work and not to some grand design.
3. The vision must be understandable: "No one can communicate a vision that takes two pages... or is too full of numbers and jargon." It has to stick in the mind.
4. The leader must live the vision: "He, or she, must not only believe in it but must be seen to believe in it.... The total pragmatist cannot be a transforming leader."
5. The leader must remember that the vision will be the work of others: Otherwise, the vision will stay just a dream. "A leader with no followers is a voice in the wilderness."

Thinking like leaders

There is nothing new or radical about this quintet. The five points deserve Handy's own judgment: "simple, obvious even." The difficulty, which is considerable, lies in the delivery. Like many other gurus, Handy wants managers to think like leaders, and believes that they can: "If it happens, and in places it is happening, it will mark yet one more important discontinuity turned to advantage."

If Handy is right, organizations are going to need a great many thinking leaders: "lots of them, all over the place and not only in the center." He sees the federal organization as flat, with no more than four or five levels at the cores of their parts, which, wherever possible, will never exceed 500 people in all. That has profound consequences for managers, who will no longer progress simply by climbing the promotion ladder, gaining a rung every two or three years.

Handy recommends instead a Japanese-style route for young people. The Japanese "have a fast-track route for them, but instead of it being a vertical fast-track up through the organization, it is a horizontal fast-track, a succession of different jobs, real jobs with tough standards to be met, but all at the same level." The same system, writes Handy, can work for all ages everywhere as the flatter organization allows people to discover new abilities and new interests.

This is another example of Handy's "upside-down thinking," horizontal careers as a good thing. Not only do corporations need an inverted approach to employment,

"If the new organizations are going to succeed, and they must succeed, our managers must think like leaders."
The Age of Unreason

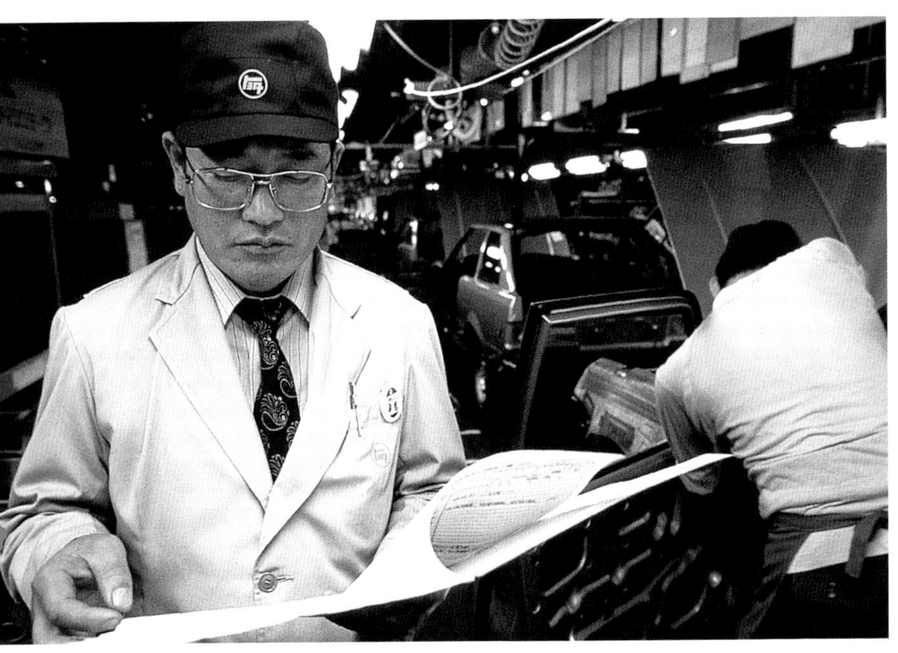

On the fast track at Toyota

Handy recommends organizations adopt the Japanese method of horizontal promotion, where employees have the opportunity of testing and improving their skills in a wide variety of roles.

they also require a new formula for success and for effectiveness: $I^3 = AV$, "where I stands for intelligence, information, and ideas, and AV means added value in cash or in kind." His formula gave Handy yet another phrase: "The Triple I Organization." This would most resemble a university, and not the traditional corporation, as it obsessively pursued quality:

"To that end the wise organization increasingly uses smart machines, with smart people to work with them. It is interesting to note how often, already, organizations talk of their 'intellectual property.' Once again, words signal the way things are going."

Quality, affirms Handy, is not another gimmick. It is the opposite of the old "money-is-all" objectives of business: the fast buck, or the short-term bottom line of residual profit, or the medium-term earnings per share. The world has become much more competitive, and "organizations will only survive if they can guarantee quality in their goods or their services. Short-term profit at the expense of quality will lead to short-term lives."

Quality, however, does not come easily. "It needs," says Handy, "the right equipment, the right people, and the right environment" (to which one might well reply, what doesn't?). The Triple I Organization fits the bill: "Everyone is paid to think *and* to do, including the machines." The myth is that automation deskills workers. Smart organizations, however, "see the computers and their machines as aides to clever people." In a dumb organization, Handy notes, smart machines are merely attended by "sometimes very dumb people." But the hard facts of economic life, he says, will compel organizations:

- To invest in smart machines to achieve effectiveness.
- To use skilled and thinking people to get the most out of the machines.
- To pay these people more and, if possible, employ fewer of them.

More of these smart people will be women, not for egalitarian reasons, but because the smart supply will be inadequate if half the population is excluded. The most important difference, however, is that "everyone in the core will have to be a manager while at the same time no one can afford to be only a manager." Professional or technical experts will also "rapidly acquire responsibility for money, people, or projects, or all three." In the newer, higher technology firms in the US, Handy notes, the language is already reflecting this: people are called, not managers, but "team-leaders," "project heads," or "coordinators."

In this new society, "Management ceases to be a definition of a status, of a class within an organization, but [becomes] an *activity*... which can be defined, and its skills taught, learned, and developed." That process, though, cannot stop with business education and early qualifications:

> "... everyone in the core will increasingly be expected to have not only the expertise appropriate to his or her particular role but will also be required to know and understand business, to have the technical skills of analysis *and* the human skills *and* the conceptual skills, and to keep them up to date."

The culture of consent

With their new careers, their new knowledge, and their new organizations, people entering Handy's new world of business seem to have bright prospects. They become brighter still when you consider "the Culture of Consent." As Handy says, "you cannot run this sort of organization or these sort of people by command... Intelligent organizations have to be run by persuasion and by consent." This is hard work, and can be frustrating; Handy emphasizes that "the cultures of consent are not easy to run, or to work in." This is partly because the culture "puts a premium on competence – there are few hiding places in these organizations."

Handy may well exaggerate the difficulties and underestimate the human potential for overcoming them. But he is setting the stage for a message close to his heart:

that people have to be "educated and prepared" for the culture of consent. "There lies the challenge for our society."

Can that challenge be met – and will it be? Handy ends *The Age of Unreason* with six hopes, involving "work done for others," religion, "village living," early success, and "the nature of man himself and particularly of woman." In all these areas, improvement could flow: original sin exists, but so does original goodness. Handy still saw many dangers in the world of looser organizations, but thought that the looseness could encourage truly adult behavior earlier in life. "If that is so then the Age of Unreason may become an Age of Greatness." The important words are "if" and "may."

Ideas into action

- Contract out anything that can be done better and/or cheaper by others.
- Exercise control by specifying the results, not by overseeing the methods.
- Ensure that decisions are made with the advice of key subordinates and by consensus.
- Make your vision different, sensible, understandable: then live it as transforming leader.
- Use flatter organizations to allow people to discover new abilities and interests.
- Employ skilled and thinking people to get the best from investment in smart machines.
- Run the organization by persuasion and by consent, putting a premium on competence.

The discovery of paradox

Handy dates to his boyhood the discovery that paradox is a necessity in life. A motto with a golfing metaphor hung in his bedroom: "Life goes, you see, to golf's own ditty: Without the rough there'd be no pretty."

In later years, Handy recognized this as his first, if subliminal, introduction to the importance of paradox. The religious upbringing inevitable for an archdeacon's son did the rest.

Handy was taught that God's great gift to mankind is choice. That, he eventually saw, was itself a paradox, "because the freedom to choose implies the freedom to choose wrongly, to sin." You could not have one without the other. He came to realize that paradox was what made life interesting. "If everything was an unmixed blessing… there would be no need for change or movement. Offer me a heaven without paradox and I will opt for hell."

That line of thought culminated in a revelation for Handy: "Life will never be easy, nor perfectible, nor completely predictable." The trail of paradox led from religion to practical affairs, as Handy discovered when he was a young executive working for Shell in South Malaysia. "Young, enthusiastic and, I suppose, naive," he was negotiating an agency agreement with a Chinese dealer. They shook hands on the deal, "drank the ritual cups of tea," and then Handy took out the official company agreement and filled the form with the relevant figures, ready for signature.

The somewhat alarmed dealer asked why a form was necessary, and protested: "If you think that I am going to sign that you are very much mistaken." If they had agreed the figures, why did Handy want a legal contract? It made the dealer suspicious. Had Shell got more than him from the agreement? In the 1990s, Handy still recalled the Chinese man's words:

> "In my culture a good agreement is self-enforcing because both parties go away smiling and are happy to see that each of us is smiling. If one smiles and the other scowls, the agreement will not stick, lawyers or no lawyers."

Handy found that the Chinese contract embodies a crucial principle. "It was about the importance of compromise as a prerequisite of progress." It rested on a basic paradox: "Both sides have to concede for both to win." Just as the possibility of sin is necessary for the pursuit of virtue, so accepting some loss led to optimum profit. "We have no chance of managing the paradoxes," wrote Handy, "if we are not prepared to give up something, if we are not willing to bet on the future and if we cannot find it in ourselves to take a risk with people."

"Living with paradox is not comfortable nor easy. It can be like walking in a dark wood on a moonless night. It is an eerie and, at times, a frightening experience."
The Empty Raincoat

That thought and its infinite number of variations led him away from dogmatism and toward his basic attitude: to challenge all dogma, but to recognize whatever value exists, even in ideas and practices that are plainly contradictory.

4

Managing the paradoxes

Why human beings are not designed to be "empty raincoats, nameless numbers on a payroll" • Employing half the people at twice the pay and three times the productivity • **The pressures of the Nine Paradoxes** • Averting disaster by adopting change before the "Sigmoid Curve" reaches its peak • **Winning the equal benefits of the "Chinese Contract"** • The "Trinitarian" thinking of Liberty, Equality, and Fraternity • **Using "inside-out" or "upside-down" thought to challenge the conventional wisdom**

Handy has had the rare satisfaction of seeing many of his prophecies come true, but not to his comfort. The predicted changes in the world of work have created "much more fundamental, confusing, and distressing" results than he expected. He has diagnosed the main cause:

> "Part of the confusion stems from our pursuit of efficiency and economic growth... In the pursuit of these goals we can be tempted to forget that it is we, as individual men and women, who should be the measure of all things...."

Here, Handy is expressing the distaste of the intellectual puritan for the ethic of the mass-market economy. The passage is from *The Empty Raincoat*, published in 1994. Why the odd title? It comes from part of a sculpture that Handy saw in Minneapolis: a bronze raincoat, standing upright but with no one wearing it. Human beings, Handy concludes, "were not designed to be empty raincoats, nameless numbers on a payroll...."

His central thrust remains unchanged. Organizations will become "smaller and bigger simultaneously, flatter, and more flexible." People will have to make things happen, rather than wait for them to happen. But Handy is left with the paradox that "the new freedoms... often mean less equality and more misery."

Handy states that many jobs have been priced out of existence in the industrialized world. Only people from poorer backgrounds will take these jobs (as many Latinos have in the US). But even good jobs have their drawbacks. Large corporations are pursuing the policy: "$\frac{1}{2}$ x 2 x 3 = P." For profit, they employ half the people at twice the pay and three times the productivity. So half the staff lose their jobs, and the other half work so hard that they can neither enjoy their families nor avoid burnout in a mere 30 years.

Handy is convinced that there has to be "more to life than winning or we should nearly all be losers." Looking around, he saw that management and control were breaking down, and that "The new world order looks very likely to end in disorder." He no longer believed in "a Theory of Everything," or in "the possibility of perfection." Such a belief was always odd for a rational observer of human affairs. But Handy now saw that scientists themselves had undermined "the myth of science, the idea that everything could be understood, predicted, and therefore managed." On the contrary, society was evolving through the pressures of nine paradoxes.

The nine paradoxes

Handy's first paradox is intelligence. He observes, rightly enough, that brainpower has taken over from fixed assets and mobile muscle as the prime means of production. Intelligence is thus "the new form of property." But this form behaves paradoxically, like no other property.

You cannot redistribute or bequeath intelligence: you cannot own somebody else's. Handy also cites management pioneer Peter Drucker: "The means of production can no longer be owned by the people who think they own the business." Intelligence, moreover, is also extraordinarily difficult to tax. Handy's insight seems to promise a more open society, with low-cost entry. Yet it also carries a threat: that society will be divided into a new set of haves and have-nots, separated by intelligence.

The second paradox is that of work. Handy says that "enforced idleness seems to be the price we are paying for improved efficiency." The paradox is that "organizations want the most work for the least money while individuals typically want the most money for the least work." Handy points to the irony that "the more you price work, the less paid work gets done, because so much of it [like small home repairs] is not now worth the cost." That is the inevitable result of the pursuit of higher productivity, which is Handy's third paradox.

"Productivity means ever more and ever better work from ever fewer people." Handy recognizes that the age-old process of improving efficiency ultimately benefited the workers, so long as jobs were available. "This time, however, the new growth structure for work is the do-it-yourself economy." People displaced from organizations do their own thing: their output is invisible, but increasing all the time. Managements have encouraged specialization and efficiency, but have in consequence "priced some of that new work out of existence." Handy admits that the resulting joblessness is "a fallout from progress," but calls it one of the most uncomfortable modern paradoxes.

Time – the fourth paradox – is familiar to everybody: "we never seem to have enough time, yet there has never been so much time available to us." Despite longer lives, automation, part-time work, flexitime, and so on, the average American now works the equivalent of an extra month per year compared to two decades ago. "Time turns out to be a confusing commodity," writes Handy. "Some people will spend money to save their time, others will spend their time to save money." As for organizations, they want fewer people working longer to save money, while individuals agree to work longer because they want money: "The paradox is that they seem to know it is stupid."

The fifth paradox – riches – is that economic growth depends on increasing numbers buying increasing quantities of goods and services. But the rich populations, which can afford to buy, are declining in numbers, while the poor nations cannot take their place until they have the know-how and capital needed to export to the rich. "Ultimately, therefore, we will have to invest in our potential competitors in order to fuel our own growth." Handy, back to his puritan vein, offers another, weaker paradox: the growth that society needs depends more and more on "a climate of envy," which increases social divisiveness.

With the sixth paradox – organizations – Handy is on stronger ground, and ground that he has made his own. Organizations are beset by the need to reconcile opposites, where they once could choose between them. Handy cites global yet local, small yet big, centralized yet decentralized, planned yet flexible, differentiated yet integrated, and so on. He argues: "The organizations of the future may not be recognizable as such.... The challenge for tomorrow's leaders is to manage an organization that is not there in any sense which we are used to." It will be an organizing organization, not an employing one.

Age, the seventh paradox, is "that every generation perceives itself as justifiably different from its predecessor, but plans as if its successor generation will be the same as them." This assumption has been thrown out of the window, according to Handy. Conventional jobs and careers will be scarcer, working lives will begin later and end earlier; "education will have to be more prolonged, if not indefinite"; women will be in paid work for most of their lives; child rearing and learning will involve both sexes; and values and principles will change as the roles of the sexes change.

The eighth paradox, that of the individual, is that people are being encouraged as never before to express their individuality, but "Looking up... at these office blocks in every city... one has to wonder how much room there is for

'I' amid the filing cabinets and the terminals." Handy is expressing another paradox of the organization. It requires teamwork, which means working together for the common good, while simultaneously expecting team members to be self-managing and motivating individuals. Handy has wider worries about the future of belonging: "Who will be the 'We' to whom we would want to belong?"

The ninth paradox is that of justice. People expect society to treat them fairly, to give them what they deserve, and to be impartial. Handy becomes apocalyptic about the prospects for a society that is perceived to be unjust: "... there will be no good reason for anything other than selfishness. Such a society is doomed, in the end, to destroy itself." Thus the debatable view of the prophet, but the paradox is firmly based. Capitalism thrives on the principle that those who achieve most should get most:

> "But it will not long be credible or tolerated if it ignores its opponent. To put it another way, capitalism depends on the fundamental principle of inequality – some may do better than others – but will only be acceptable in the long term in a democracy if most people have an equal chance to aspire to that inequality. It is a paradox which we cannot afford to ignore."

Handy develops strong ideas for ways of resolving his paradoxes, although his prophecies are not watertight. He writes: "Governments seem surprised when each recovery soaks up fewer of the unemployed." But, as the millennium ended, this phenomenon was no longer relevant in the US, and less relevant in Britain. That, however, does not remove the need to live with contradictions and simultaneous opposites. Handy offers three methods of doing so: the Sigmoid Curve, the Doughnut Principle (see pp. 89–101), which is the most famous, and the Chinese Contract.

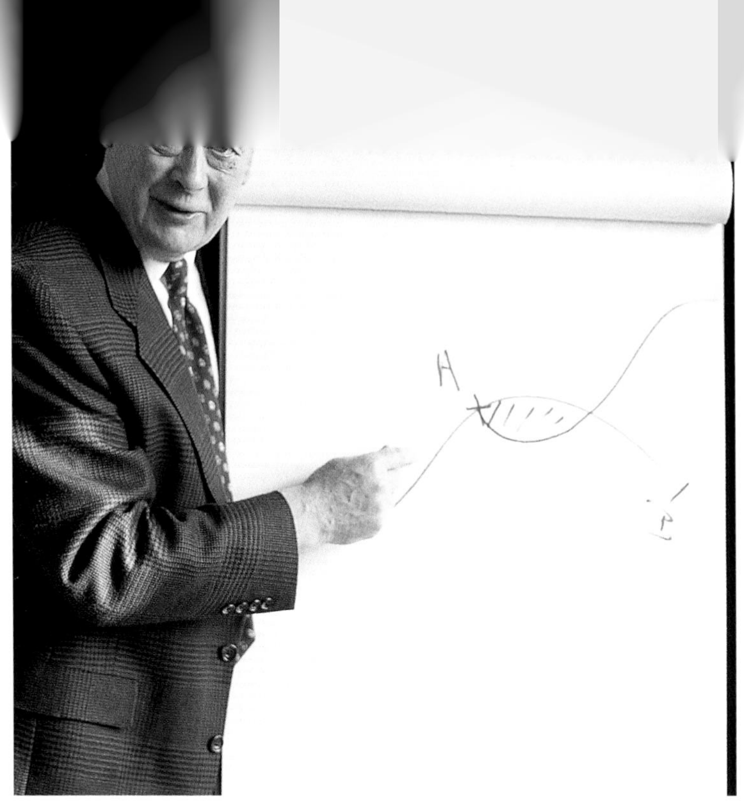

Explaining the Sigmoid Curve
Charles Handy explains to managers that the secret of continued growth is to take a new course at point A, before reaching a peak of success, and well before disaster looms at point B.

The Sigmoid Curve

The Sigmoid Curve is S-shaped (see also p. 85). It describes a familiar pattern, that of life itself. "We start slowly, experimentally, and falteringly, we wax and then we wane." Progress along the curve has increased. "What used to take decades, even generations, now takes years, even months." The secret of constant growth, Handy says, is to start a new curve just before the crest of the old. But that is when everything seems fine: "It would be folly to change when the current recipes are working so well."

The true folly is exposed when the curve continues around the bend and below the crest, where "you are looking disaster in the face." Now, huge effort is required to remedy the situation and get back on an upward trend – a second growth curve – because resources, energies, morale, and credibility are all low. Upheaval follows. At this point:

> "... institutions invariably start the changing process... by bringing in new people, because only people who are new to the situation will have the credibility and the different vision to lift the place back onto the second curve."

The tough question is: "How do we know where we are on the first curve?" Handy advises organizations to assume that their present strategies will need to be replaced within two to three years, and that product life cycles are shorter than they were. Even if this assumption proves to be wrong, no harm has been done. The organization has merely explored the new possibilities without making major commitments, and the "discipline of the second curve" is useful in itself, keeping one skeptical, curious, and inventive.

In fact, Handy is contradicted by many examples of companies that have changed winning strategies fatally and unnecessarily. Moreover, major commitments are often required earlier than he suggests. But it remains true that "nothing lasts forever or was there forever," although many managers act as if it does. He cites the MIT professor Peter

"It is one of the paradoxes of success that the things and the ways which got you where you are, are seldom the things to keep you there."
The Empty Raincoat

Senge for pointing out the importance of "mental maps," the fixed ideas that everybody carries around. "We need to check that these assumptions are still valid, because they lock us into our existing curve."

Second-curve thinking, Handy insists, comes most naturally from the second generation. Elders should entrust "curvilinear thinking" to younger people who "can see more clearly where the first curve is heading and what the next curve might look like." The danger is that their visionary thinking will be obstructed by the powerful elders.

> "The thinking, however, is only part of it. There needs to be the commitment to carry it through, to endure the early dip before the curve climbs upward, to live with the first curve while the second one develops. These things cannot be done by outsiders. To manage a paradox, you need to live with it as well as analyze it."

The Chinese Contract

A further way to handle paradox is covered by another of Handy's mysterious titles: the "Chinese Contract." Agreements made in Asia are supposed to rest, not on the letter of a legal contract, but on reaching a compromise that suits the interests of both parties. He notes that "the morality of compromise" sounds contradictory. Compromise, especially on "principles," is usually seen as weakness. Handy argues that strong people always know when to compromise and that "all principles can be compromised to serve a greater principle."

If this sounds odd coming from a religious man, Handy has a convincing explanation. Most dilemmas are not a choice between right and wrong, but between two conflicting rights: "I want to spend more time on my work, *and* with my family." Similarly, managers want to give their employees freedom and keep control over their activities. Businesses are always confronting the paradox of conflicting rights. Investment, for example, "involves taking something from today to improve tomorrow." So how far should you short-change or compromise the present to benefit the future?

Third-angle thinking

Handy urges that you should seek the answers to such questions through "Trinitarian," or third-angle thinking. The name is another of his potent analogies. The trinity is that of the French Revolution: liberty, equality, and fraternity. The first two are in conflict, but adding fraternity reconciles them; likewise, you should always be on the lookout for another approach to resolving conflict – the third angle. The idea brings Handy's social ethics to the fore: "if money is so divisive, why not de-monetarize society" by making more of the good necessities of life free to all?

He does not answer his own question, which raises far weightier economic issues than the divisiveness of money. But he does make a strong case for challenging Western cultural traditions along the lines of the "Chinese Contract":

- Reject the idea that winning necessarily means that someone loses.
- Regard compromise as a sign of strength.
- Seek a good agreement, not a good lawyer.
- Reject the idea that if you look after the present, the future will look after itself.

The four pieces of advice are excellent. But neither the Chinese Contract nor the Sigmoid Curve is as powerful as the Doughnut Principle. The doughnut Handy refers to is an inverted ring doughnut, with the "middle" representing a core of essential activities surrounded by discretionary space. It is another example of the "inside-out" or "upside-down" thinking, central to Handy's later writings, that leads him, always alert for paradox, to challenge so much conventional business wisdom.

He quotes John Akers, who just before leaving the IBM leadership complained that: "The average IBM-er has lost sight of the reasons for his company's existence. IBM exists to provide a basic return on invested capital to the shareholders." Handy is baffled by the persistence of this wrong premise and its false assumptions, which are denied by his own experience in business and by logic. His view on the purpose of business is utterly different:

> "The principal purpose of a company… is to make a profit in order to continue to do things or make things, and to do so ever better and more abundantly."

Saying that profit is a means to an end, not an end in itself, makes a serious moral point; the opposite view, according to St. Augustine, "is one of the worst of sins." Yet Handy's own words on the subject are surprising. If the principal purpose of a company is to make a profit, why undertake one activity rather than another? Profit is neither an end nor a means, but an end result, the reward that flows from doing or making, better and more abundantly, what you want to do or make – as the favorite jargon of the year 2000 would say, by optimizing customer satisfaction.

Handy does recognize this truth later on in *The Empty Raincoat*, when he says: "A company will only be allowed to survive as long as it is doing something useful, at a cost which people can afford, and it must generate enough funds for… continued growth and development." This "existential" company combines selfishness with public contribution (another resolved paradox) within the "hexagon contract." This is a form of Chinese Contract, implicitly agreed by a company's six different stakeholders: the financiers, employees, and suppliers most obviously, but also the customers, the environment, and society as a whole.

Most of these stakeholders, says Handy, are likely to have "a vested interest in immortality," seeking perpetuity for a business that will continue only for as long as it is good. The conflict between satisfying the interests of investors (who want the highest financial returns) and employees (who want the highest possible reward) is tackled by the existential company that lives for its own virtuous purpose: for example, growing "better not bigger." That, Handy writes, is one definition of a purpose, one way to grow, "one recipe for immortality."

Institutional immortality

Handy is forced to concede, however, that few corporations are following his recipe. "In a business, quarterly reports and an average lifespan of 40 years for big companies tend to put immortality on the back burner." Handy says that boardrooms do not trust numbers more than four or five years ahead. Such numbers, anyway, are bound to be deeply untrustworthy. But Handy thinks this short-sightedness ill-founded; institutions, he declares, can be immortal.

"The Mitsui Corporation and my old Oxford college are both over 600 years old, both still going strong and thinking far," according to Handy, who adds, rather mystifyingly: "You only look ahead as far as you can look back." His "fragile" hopes are that job-hopping will become more perilous, and shareholders less powerful, and that the "virtues of membership" will be rediscovered. Then "the corporate world may see a desire for permanence creep in again" – a hope that reads unconvincingly against the millennial background of megamergers and demergers.

The recipe for immortality, though, has to be read in the context of the point where *The Empty Raincoat* begins: "that there is no perfect solution to anything, and that no one can predict the ultimate effect of any action." There is neither certainty nor sure authority – the paradoxes are too complicated for that. Yet Handy offers a certain and authoritative conclusion: "We have to put these principles into practice, in our work and in our lives." Offering a solution when there is no solution is Handy's own paradox.

Ideas into action

- Assume that your present strategies will need replacing in two to three years' time.
- Entrust planning radical "second-curve" strategy to the younger generation.
- Be prepared to compromise in the interests of reaching a better solution.
- Always look out for another approach to resolving conflict – the third angle.
- Be alert for paradox, and use its contradictions as a springboard for success.
- Satisfy all six stakeholders: financiers, employees, suppliers, customers, the environment, and society.
- Build a company with a recipe for immortality – like being better, not bigger.

Organizing the organization

There is no one perfect way of organizing a business. Whatever method you choose, it must combine control with flexibility to be successful. Structure groups for optimum communication and balance of roles, and for maximum efficiency avoid creating too many hierarchical levels. Above all, renew the organization regularly to avert decline and fall.

Designing the setup

Always take time and care to plan your organization, whether you are setting up a small unit or a whole business. An effective setup greatly increases the chances of success.

Follow the Goldilocks principle – "not too little, not too much, but just right." That means having no more people than the task requires, but also building in plenty of flexibility. To help you plan the structure of the group and its personnel, make sure you know the answers to the following questions:

- What is the prime purpose of this organization?
- What are the subobjectives?
- What tasks must be performed to meet the aims?
- What skills do the tasks require?
- How many people are needed to deliver the skills?
- What are the natural groupings of people?
- What are the desired/required results?
- What is the optimum size – that is, the minimum number consistent with obtaining the desired results?

Once you have planned the setup according to your answers, you must ensure that everybody knows what their responsibilities are, to whom they are responsible, and who makes the final decisions.

How an organization grows

Organizations tend to grow from simple forms to complex ones. They must mutate to cope with changing demands. As an organization matures and grows larger, it passes through four distinct evolutionary phases, each ended by a revolutionary or crisis stage, which enables it to move on to the next evolutionary phase. Your organization will pass – or will have passed – through the same stages of evolution.

The Four Phases of Growth
1 Growth through creativity, ending in crisis of leadership.
2 Growth through direction, ending in crisis of autonomy.
3 Growth through delegation, ending in crisis of control.
4 Growth through coordination, ending in crisis of red tape.

Preventing stasis

During phase four, more and more processes are put into place to exercise control (over everything from spending to planning), to find out what's happening, and to keep efficient records. These good intentions rapidly develop into bad practices: filling in forms, following written procedures, getting authorizations, endless meetings. The organization becomes a static bureaucracy.

To break the stranglehold of red tape and to prevent it from recurring, always remember KISS (Keep It Simple Stupid), and follow antibureaucratic practices at all times.

Counter Bureaucracy

- Have an annual spring cleaning, using the principles of zero-based budgeting: every administrative procedure and expenditure is unnecessary unless proved otherwise.
- Wherever possible, use trust instead of controls.
- Authorize people to miss meetings where they cannot make a contribution and to challenge the value of any forms and reports.
- Reward administrative departments for task-force successes in streamlining and eliminating procedures.
- Reward good ideas that cut red tape and administrative costs.
- Be radical and courageous in seeking reforms.

The rule book of retailer Nordstrom begins on a single page saying "Use your best judgment at all times." The second page says "There are no other rules." Both rules are excellent.

1 Making groups work

How well your organization works depends on the effectiveness of its groups – both internally and in their interactions with other groups. Make sure any group you set up communicates well and is composed of members who together provide a good balance of roles.

Communicating with others

Handy lists three basic patterns for intergroup relationships. In the first you communicate primarily with the person in the center; in the second you communicate with each other in sequence; and in the third you link up with whomever you want whenever you need.

The Three Group Communication Patterns		
1 Wheel center-led	**2 Circle** sequential	**3 Web** participative

Using the web pattern

The web is the most effective communication pattern you can use. It is participative, involving, and improves quality, although, warns Handy, it tends to disintegrate into a wheel under time pressure. "In complex open-ended problems," Handy reports, "the web is the most likely to reach the best solution." In business today, complex open-ended problems abound. So making the web work is the acid test of a good group, and of your effectiveness as a manager.

Use the wheel only when speedy results matter even more than quality, bearing in mind that much depends on the peerless leader at the hub. Avoid using the circular pattern at all times. It is slow, unsatisfying, inflexible, and uncoordinated.

Picking group members

Whether the group is permanent (a department, say) or temporary (a task force), and whatever communication pattern it uses, you need to ensure that you select members to fill particular roles. This means more than making sure that different kinds of technical or professional competence are represented. According to team expert Murray Belbin, in most circumstances the fulfillment of eight key roles is essential to effective group performance.

The Eight Key Roles in a Group
1 Chairman: coordinates the group's work.
2 Shaper: drives the group and task forward.
3 Plant: comes up with the new ideas.
4 Monitor-evaluator: analyzes plans and performance.
5 Resource-investigator: provides internal and external contacts.
6 Company worker: organizes tasks and schedules.
7 Team worker: holds group together by providing support.
8 Finisher: makes things happen – and on time.

Make sure that every role is covered, but do not have too many people in the same role. Also, do not ask people to play roles to which they are unsuited by nature. Think carefully about your own role, too. If you are in charge, avoid combining the roles of chairman and shaper: you cannot perform both roles simultaneously. The chairman has to be objective, listen to everybody, and work through others; the shaper must be single-minded and forceful.

Testing effectiveness

Once your group is up and running, check its effectiveness (and your own), by testing it with the following questions:

- Do people share their information fully and freely?
- Do they tell the factual truth at all times?
- Do they face problems as a group, not as subgroups?
- Do they seek "Win/Win" solutions, with no losers?
- Are they always active and alert in group activities?
- Do they put contribution ahead of self-promotion?
- Do they display emotions as well as logic?

If the answers are negative, so will be the results. If there are faults, hold a team meeting and bring the defects into the open. Where individuals are at fault, confront them face-to-face. Publish an agreed code of conduct and insist that everybody adheres to it.

2 Organizing control

Lines of command are basic to organizational control. Whether you run the lines down through functions, territories, businesses, or products, each hierarchical layer is broader than its predecessor. For optimum efficiency and flexibility create as few layers as possible.

Increasing the span of control

As your unit grows, instead of adding hierarchical levels, increase the "span of control" at each existing level: in other words, increase the number of people who report to each superior. By creating maximum spans you give people maximum responsibility.

If the work of people reporting to you interlocks, you should not supervise more than six of them. If their work is independent, though, spans can be very much wider. Jack Welch at General Electric has built a fabulous management record with a dozen or more independent operating heads reporting directly to him.

Promoting flexibility and creativity

Handy quotes two experts who say that most organizations need only five hierarchical levels, seven if really large. But management guru James Champy says that three will suffice for any organization if you adopt a control structure that includes external expertise.

Champy's Structure	
Three-layer hierarchy	**Outside the hierarchy**
Enterprise managers People/process managers Self-managers	Expertise managers

In his ideal, enterprise managers make the final decisions. They are advised by the people-process managers, who implement the decisions and are responsible for the self-managers – the staff and line workers. The expertise managers outside the hierarchy provide the indispensable services, from finance to training. This structure depends on true delegation, and is inherently creative and flexible – which is what you want your unit to be for greatest effectiveness.

3 Beating the life cycle

Organizations tend to follow a life cycle in which their rise to achievement and wealth is followed by decline and fall. Avoid this fate by renewing your group while it is still strong and growing.

Renewing the organization

Timely renewal of an organization is rare. It does not have to be. To master the timing, apply the Sigmoid Curve (see p. 73) to your group.

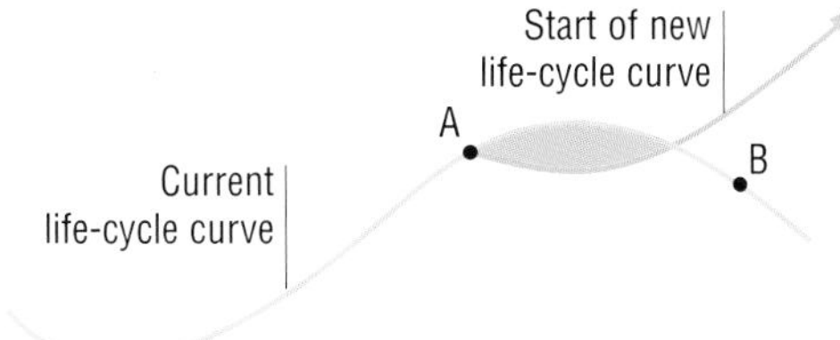

Master the curve
Begin a new iniative when you reach point A on your existing curve to avoid certain failure at point B.

Draw your own S-shaped life-cycle curve. Work out where you (or your organization) are along the curve by checking the validity of your key assumptions, and mark that position with an X. You will probably find you are further along than you would have thought.

Do not wait for bad results before instigating change. By the time you reach point B on the curve, resources will be depleted, energies will be low, and people will be depressed. Avoid decline completely by renewing your business or group on a regular basis.

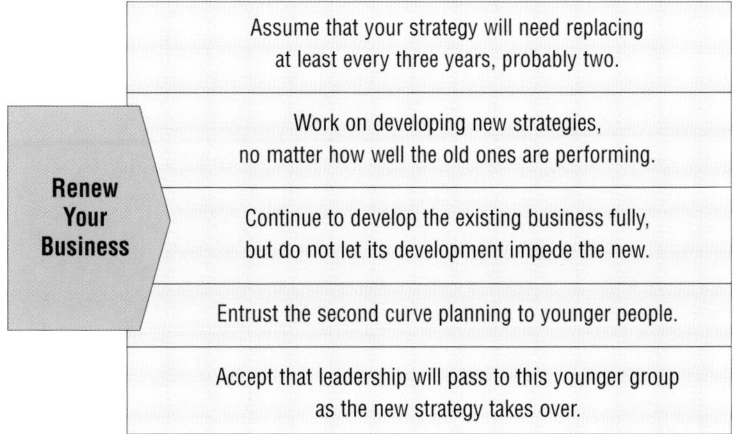

Renew Your Business
Assume that your strategy will need replacing at least every three years, probably two.
Work on developing new strategies, no matter how well the old ones are performing.
Continue to develop the existing business fully, but do not let its development impede the new.
Entrust the second curve planning to younger people.
Accept that leadership will pass to this younger group as the new strategy takes over.

Adopting a portfolio career

Handy's discovery of the need for a new approach to work can be traced back to the early 1960s, when he was appointed to a job with Shell as the Regional Coordinator Marketing (Oil) Mediterranean Region.

Handy commented later: "My friends were impressed, but they did not know the reality. The reality was a three-page job description outlining my duties, but the hard truth was contained in the final paragraph: 'Authority to initiate expenditure up to a maximum of $15.'"

In the terms that Handy coined later – those of the "inside-out doughnut" – "the job was all core and no space." His role was predictable, planned, and controlled, and designed to spare the organization any surprises. Handy found his work dull and frustrating. He could not express himself, he could not make a difference, he was not empowered: "My memoranda went from my role – MK/32 – not from me. I was merely a 'temporary role occupant.'"

Switching to another of his metaphors, Handy remarks that he felt like an "empty raincoat." Leaving Shell as soon as he could, he resumed his search for the perfect job: interesting, exciting, rewarding him with money, travel, and pride, complete with pleasing colleagues and location. He never found it. But there was a doughnut solution:

> "If I adopted a 'portfolio' approach to life, meaning that I saw my life as a collection of different groups and activities, of bits and pieces of work, like a stock portfolio, I could get different things from different bits. A part of that portfolio would be 'core,' providing the essential wherewithal for life, but it would be balanced by work done purely for interest or for a cause, or because it would stretch me personally, or simply because it was fascinating or fun."

That meant saying goodbye to offers of 70-hour-a-week jobs that would have absorbed most of his time. Handy put together a package of different kinds of work, a work portfolio: "My life now is doughnut-shaped." He became a laboratory for testing

"The concept of balancing a core and a bounded space is crucial to a proper understanding of most of life.... It is a way of being an instrument of society but also a free individual."
The Empty Raincoat

his own theory, and it works: "I can now even specify the amount of days which I am prepared to allocate to core activities and the amount left over for personal space." Handy had discovered a new principle of organizing work for the new society.

The new principle, Handy originally thought, would be applied primarily in the Third Age, "the time for a second life." While this could be a continuation of the Second Age, "the time of main endeavor," it might be "something very different." Doing nothing, writes Handy, is no longer a realistic Third Age option. Having a portfolio is realistic, and many people in mid-life are now emulating Handy in this respect.

Even more interesting, Second Age people are also opting for plural careers, while companies are pluralizing and empowering their managers. Today's young managers would not be Regional Coordinator Marketing (Oil) Mediterranean Region, or an MK/2 – thanks partly to Handy.

5

Living in a doughnut

Applying the "Doughnut Principle" to jobs and organizations • The distinction between getting it wrong and not getting it right • **Developing the "portfolio career"** • Using different tasks and groups to bring out different talents • **Why the vertically integrated company is obsolete** • Laying out the doughnut organization • **How to avoid overdoing the core activities** • How organizations are structuring themselves into minimalist shapes • **Putting how you use time ahead of how much time you use**

Perhaps the greatest contribution in *The Empty Raincoat* is Handy's second pathway through paradox, the concept of the doughnut, the ring doughnut with a hole in the middle. He turns the doughnut (or "donut") inside out, with a core that "contains all the things which have to be done in (your) job or role if you are not to fail." The space around and beyond the core provides "our opportunity to make a difference, to go beyond the bounds of duty, to live up to our full potential."

This use of the doughnut metaphor for individuals has been less influential than its application to institutions. Organizations, just as Handy predicted, "have come to realize that they have their essential core... of necessary jobs and necessary people, a core which is surrounded by an open, flexible space which they fill with flexible workers and flexible supply contracts." Handy thus gives expression to a powerful corporate trend, in which companies "outsource" whatever they can.

The Doughnut Principle applies to jobs as well as to organizations. "In the past, jobs used to be all core, certainly at the lower levels, because too much discretion meant too much unpredictability." In such cases, the doughnut, because it is all core and no space, leaves no room for self-expression, no space to make a difference, no empowerment.

Handy experienced this discomfort in person when working for Shell as Regional Coordinator Marketing (Oil)

"The doughnut image is a conceptual way of relating duty to a fuller responsibility in every institution or group in society."
The Empty Raincoat

Mediterranean Region (see pp. 86–87). With a job that is "all core and no space," the result is dullness and frustration. But the opposite extreme, all space and no core, also has grave disadvantages. In a job such as that of a pastor, "there is no end, no way in which you can look back and say, 'It was a great year,' because it could always have been greater." But that must surely be true of any job.

Types of error

However, Handy wants to make the point that empowerment has gone too far, that being without a boundary is never enough. Even entrepreneurs need targets and limits: working all hours does not balance the doughnut. Another disadvantage of more space is having more room for "Type 2 error." Handy makes a vital distinction between getting it wrong (Type 1 error) and not getting it right (Type 2), which means that "the full possibilities have not been exploited or developed: enough was not enough."

Type 2 has become more important. Management, says Handy, was easier when the priority was to check for only Type 1 errors. Managing thus became merely administration, and managers never needed to explore the first statement in these familiar words from the old Anglican prayer book:

> "We have left undone those things which we ought to have done [Type 2]... and we have done those things which we ought not to have done [Type 1]."

Leaner and flatter organizations, in Handy's view, have given people more space at the price of a new Type 2 burden: "the things we could have done but didn't." The extra space in the doughnut brings extra responsibility. He sees acceptance of this truth as the way to "a truly free society." That is surely beyond man's reach. But the aspiration reveals the moral purpose underlying all Handy's work, and which clearly lies beneath the following question:

> "Some people make their work the whole of their life. That necessary core of the job fills the whole doughnut, leaving little or no space for anything else. Are they right or wise?"

Handy does not provide a clear answer. Some people, he notes, suggest that those who seek personal fulfillment in demanding business jobs will be disappointed. Others think that the business of creating wealth can and should fulfill people's aspirations. Handy offers his doughnut as a bridge between the opposites: if your current job does not provide your "existential development," fill the empty spaces in your personal doughnut somewhere else.

The portfolio career

Here, Handy is developing perhaps his most famous idea: the "portfolio career." More and more people are following in his footsteps by leaving full-time employment, as Handy did at 50, and working for several employers, or clients, in different guises. The portfolio principle, however, is compatible with full-time employment, if you have the good fortune to work for an organization that provides different kinds of work within its walls. People can than join a number of different doughnuts:

> "Wise organizations recognize the advantages of these internal portfolios. Different tasks and different groups bring out different talents in the individual; they confront him or her with different experiences."

This portfolio pattern is, in fact, appearing in large organizations. It is happening as a response to market and other trends, and to the demands of competition, rather than as a result of any sociological upheaval. Handy points to the death of the old organization chart: today's have "circles and amoebalike blobs where... boxes used to be." The boundaries have become fuzzy as well, "with customers, suppliers, and allied organizations linked into a varying 'network organization.'"

Handy was among the first observers to discern a "new shape of work." He saw it centering around small operations, mostly in services, which would use outsiders or portfolio workers to supplement a small core of key people. This is a "doughnut organization." The vertically integrated company which wanted to own and run everything internally is obsolete. Rather, every organization these days has its smaller core and its surrounding partnerships: traditional suppliers, independent professionals, joint venture partners, and so on.

Handy is always sharp-eyed about drawbacks. He sees a danger in bonding the partners so tightly that they become part of the core, and warns that the flexibility which is the whole point of the doughnut can disappear. He calls for flexible contracts, and recommends never tying more than 30 percent of capacity or requirements to a single partner. He also stresses that managing doughnuts is a new challenge for organizations:

> "It is a challenge because one is managing the doughnut and its different spaces, rather than the person... It is no longer the manager and the managed, but the designer of the doughnut and the occupant; a different relationship, built more on trust and mutual respect than on control."

Handy gives the example of Ricardo Semler, the president of Semco, a Brazilian engineering business, who has pioneered a form of doughnut organization. The company has a group of counselors in the middle of the business, while all the other employees, known as "partners" or "associates," live in the outer space. They all occupy smaller doughnuts, held together by coordinators. But what can be achieved at Semco, which is privately owned and relatively small, is obviously easier than it would be in larger, public organizations.

But larger organizations are trying. As Handy says: "Organizations everywhere are being 'reinvented' or 're-engineered'… breaking down, or rather blowing up their functions and their old ways of working, and… regrouping people, equipment, and systems around a particular task."

Ricardo Semler

Semler's maverick reorganization of his engineering business, Semco, into a participative venture company has made it one of the most advanced and best-known companies in Latin America.

He fits these new groupings into his doughnut metaphor by calling their specific objectives, rules, and duties the "core," with the surrounding space described as the discretionary freedom to complete the task "in the way they think best."

The doughnut organization may even be laid out physically to suit the metaphor. "The center no longer dominates from a headquarters tower block. It is smaller and more clublike, with outlying or satellite offices around the country." Handy believes that the present nomadic lifestyle of many modern executives, who spend little time in the office or at home, could be mirrored by corporate premises. He cites research by Frank Becker that envisions a central doughnut, a computer-equipped home office, and a satellite office in suburbia.

Overdoing the core

But these predictions are less important to Handy than a sermon. He believes that people and organizations overdo the core. Few individuals "need as much as they think they do, or as much security as they hanker after. Organizations build bigger cores than they need, and impose bigger cores on their internal doughnuts than are necessary." It is central to Handy's philosophy that: "If we do not allow people space, we cannot expect responsible behavior." Organizations must adapt to their needs.

> "For organizations the opportunity is now there to apply the doughnut principle to most of their work, devising a structure made up of muddy doughnuts, a system of interlocking double circles, in each of which the inner circle, the core, is tightly specified and controlled, as are the outer limits of authority, but where the space in the middle is to be developed."

Handy sees that anarchy can follow if the organization is lax, and its managers cannot handle the inevitable contradictions. What satisfies individuals and groups may not be advantageous to the organization. "The center cracks down, cores expand again, individuals resent the contraction of their space, and mutual resentment saps morale." The only remedy, in large doughnuts, is to develop a clear consensus about individual and corporate purposes and goals. But doughnut management is becoming an increasingly important skill because of the sheer proliferation going on inside organizations.

As Handy predicted, an increasing number of organizations are dividing their employees into "project teams, task forces, small business units, clusters, and work groups – smart words for doughnuts." The individual may even have multiple roles, say, in an operational doughnut, in an advisory one, and in another handling a temporary product assignment. Handy sees this as exciting for people, at the price of unpredictability. It is another nail in the coffin of the planned career. He notes that people are now being offered "career opportunities" instead of jobs.

Handy selects a real-life model – the advertising agency – to illustrate his view of "how we will be working tomorrow." People are organized into clusters of experts from whom task groups are selected for a particular account or campaign. "They may work on several different account groups, and the membership of the groups will flex with the demands of the work. It is a fluid-matrix organization." So is a consultancy, or the team at a medical center.

It is questionable whether these models are appropriate. How organizations arrange themselves is determined in a major way by the nature of their work. How else could you organize an advertising agency? As he says, "professionals have always worked on the principle of the doughnut." The work consists of related products, which call on some common services, but which are inherently distinct one-time projects: "flexibility and discretion had to be built in."

But if his model has weaknesses, his point does not. Such outfits, with their naturally flatter and looser structures, are being imitated, as far as possible, by larger organizations. Hierarchical ranks and disciplines are lessening in importance as flexibility and discretion become more critical for success. Organizational life is changing form. Slowly in most cases, fast in others, "organizations structure themselves into minimalist shapes."

The consequences have powerful effects outside firms. Organizations spin off insiders to join the ranks of outsiders, "most of them reluctant independents." As and when they find work, more and more spun-off individuals "are behaving as professionals always have, charging fees, not wages." In Handy's terms they are "going portfolio or going plural." He does not mean having several different kinds of work, but having several different clients.

What distinguishes these workers from in-house hired hands is that the price tag now goes on "their contribution, not their time." The value may vary from a $5 million commission, earned by a single introduction, to Handy's reward for writing *The Empty Raincoat*. As he notes wryly:

> "If I was paid by the hour at the average national wage for writing this book I would be counting my income in many tens of thousands of pounds. Sadly, the royalty advance takes no account of my time, but prices my produce at the level my publisher thinks it will fetch in the marketplace. I therefore sell my time cheaply to myself, in the hope that it will be an investment worth the making."

Knowledge workers

Applied intelligence, Handy argues, has become the crucial element, not time. Knowledge workers of all types "are obvious candidates for portfolio lives." They are no different, however, from the vast numbers of people whose members can be found all over the Yellow Pages: the fixers and makers, the craftsmen and craftswomen. Their work may be harder and longer than that of employees. "The difference is that they have more freedom to chunk their time in other ways, if they so choose."

Handy is emphatic that: "What matters now is *how* we use our time, not *how much* of that time we use." Charging by the hour is much less sensible than charging for the produce. "Those who charge for their produce can get richer by working smarter, not longer." This principle stretches beyond the individual portfolio worker. "Organizations are also latching on to the possibilities... extending the principle of produce not time to their own internal operations."

A unit, group, or person may be told: "Do this by this date; how you do it is up to you, but get it done on time and up to standard." Like the outsider, the insider gets more discretion in handling his or her time. The main difference remaining, says Handy, is that the full-time worker will have rights and entitlements that do not extend to the part-timer. He does not think that this distinction can or should last: "I have little doubt that we shall, increasingly, see both laws and best practice equalizing the benefits, proportionately, between full- and part-timers."

Another form of equalization concerns accommodation. The full-timer can go to an office. Portfolio workers, too, "need somewhere where they belong as of right." Handy is worried about the alienating effect of learning all by yourself, the loneliness of teleworking: "That asset which is yourself can atrophy in isolation." Companionship and gossip are required with people who are colleagues, not clients. Handy calls for: "Somewhere where we can exchange experience and contacts. We need a club." In the minimalist organization, the hub, he believes, "will be a clubhouse for the members of the dispersed core" – one that key portfolio workers also use.

Handy encourages portfolio workers to demand the use of a club facility as part of their fees. That deal can obviously be struck only with a company that takes a radically changed attitude to employment and to its own identity, and that regards insiders and outsiders as equally valuable. (The analogy is with a company like Dell Computer, which outsources much of its essential activity to suppliers who are regarded as part of the business.) Such an attitude is hard to avoid when, as Handy stresses, employment itself is changing, and with it the nature of organization.

For those offically inside, part of the personal doughnut will be the core, a job whose content may be written down in a job description; or, "if it's a classy organization," in a mission statement. But there is a snag. When those core activities have been completed, "you have not finished, for there is more." Handy remarks that in any job of any significance the jobholder is expected to do all that is required, and much more:

> "... to make a difference, to show responsible and appropriate initiative, to move into the empty space of the doughnut and begin to fill it up. Unfortunately, no one can tell you what you should do there because if they could they would make it part of the core. It is another organizational Catch-22. All they can tell you is the boundary of your discretion, the outer rim of the doughnut."

As Handy emphasizes, many organizations are now beset by the pressures of complexity, variety, and necessary speed of reaction. All this "makes the well-cored doughnut an impossible dream." Managers must struggle with the snag, be specific about core content, boundaries, and expected results, and follow a new philosophy of management that marks a major discontinuity. Among other things, they have to learn to forgive mistakes. Some, of course, are unforgivable, "but most are less critical than they seem at the time and can be the crux of important lessons."

The new manager

Forgiveness is asking a lot of organizations, which "are not by nature forgiving places." The organization itself, however, neither forgives nor blames: individual managers within the institution do that, heavily influenced by cultural norms, no doubt, but still acting as the final arbiters. The consequence is obvious: "The new manager must be a different manager," a person with a lot of learning to do. "The new manager must learn to specify the measures of success as well as the signs of failure, and must then allow his or her people to get on with it in their own way." The issue is whether he or she will.

In answer to such questions, Handy ends *The Empty Raincoat* with a large prophecy and a small prescription. He proclaims "the end of the age of the mass organization [which] has not been with us that long. We should not think of it as a law of nature." Nor is that necessarily bad news: "Maybe we shall be better off without it." Since Handy makes no secret of his distaste for mass organizations yet approves of so much contemporary and coming change, the cautious pessimism of his conclusion is surprising:

"We cannot wait for great visions from great people, for they are in short supply at *the end of history* [my italics]. It is up to us to light our own small fires in the darkness."

Readers who accompany Handy on what seems a hopeful journey must be puzzled to reach such a gloomy terminus. Has history really ended, and in darkness? Its trends, down the ages, have always rested on the collective, cumulative actions of individuals striving toward a brighter future. In *Beyond Certainty*, a 1995 collection of essays, Handy explains his position: "I remain optimistic about the possibilities of the future but pessimistic about our willingness to seize them." That is a final, personal paradox.

Ideas into action

- Seek and pursue the essential core of your personal and business activities.
- Unearth and prevent the unseen errors – the undone things you should have done.
- Help people to develop portfolio careers, either inside or outside the firm.
- Organize clusters of experts from whom you select task forces for specific projects.
- Employ and pay people for their results, not for the time they spend on getting them.
- Learn how to forgive mistakes and make them the crux of important lessons.
- Allow your people to get on with their work in their own way.

Organizing yourself

Charles Handy has approached his own life and career with the efficient planning of a truly modern manager. Even if you are not a "portfolio" worker, with a fee-paid, multiclient career, the portfolio principles are highly important in getting the most out of your work – and life. Learn to choose the work that suits you, and to plan your life around that choice.

Making personal choices

Developments inside companies mean that you have a wider choice than ever in the way in which you can serve an organization. Handy has identified three distinct working relationships between employees and employers.

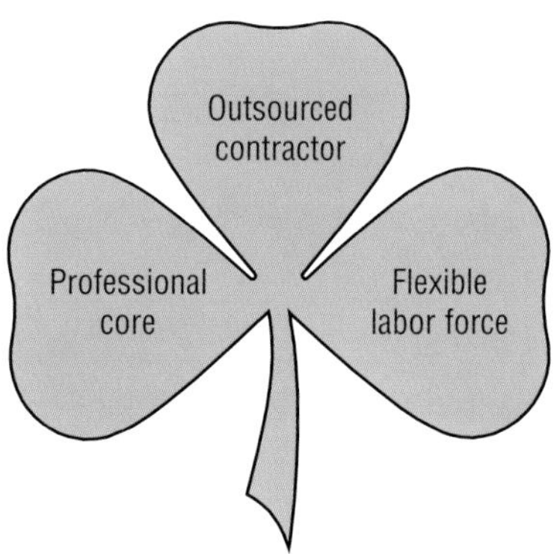

The three leaves of the shamrock

Today's organization is made up of three very different groups of people. To which group do you belong?

Choosing how to work

The choice for managers is between two leaves of the shamrock – being either a salaried member of the core or a fee-earning contributor of contracted skills. Weigh up the two options carefully before making your choice.

- As a contractor, you have the flexibility, variety, and upside potential of being your own man or woman. But your earning capacity is limited by the number of hours you can work and the fees you can charge, and you have very little security.
- As a salaried member of the core, you have greater security, considerable scope, and guaranteed rewards. But your freedom of movement and decision is outside your control.

Finding what suits

If you are undecided on your best way of working, look again at the questionnaires in Masterclass 1, and answer each proposition with yourself rather than an organization in mind.

- If you agree predominantly with the Zeus attitudes, you are either a born subordinate who needs a commanding boss, or a potential entrepreneur, a leader with the personal drive that can turn a business idea into profitable action.
- If you find you are an Apollonian, you will probably be happiest as a core professional, a salaried employee working within an organization.
- If you discover you have mainly Athenian attitudes, then you will be most suited to a highly decentralized, participative organization, or to your own consultancy-type operation.
- If you find you have primarily Dionysian characteristics, then you are a natural freelancer and heretic.

The ten commandments

If you believe after doing this exercise that you are in the wrong organization, think of moving. "Have skill, will travel" is the right motto to adopt. You should also consider moving if the company disobeys the 10 commandments of modern management.

Obey the 10 Commandments

1 Welcome new ideas – especially from below.
2 Insist that people need approval from only one level.
3 Praise when praise is due and only criticize constructively.
4 Encourage open debate ending in consensus.
5 Treat problems as opportunities.
6 Use trust, not supervision, as the main control.
7 Operate a "freedom of information" policy.
8 Institute change after consultation with those affected.
9 Take, announce, implement unpleasant decisions in person.
10 Share knowledge with others and share theirs.

1 Balancing your life

Handy bases his life on the Doughnut Principle. That means achieving a proper balance between mandatory and optional activities, between work and leisure. Getting the balance right is much more likely if you organize the doughnut efficiently.

Applying the doughnut

The inside-out doughnut is one of Handy's key ideas. The concept can be applied to your work alone, or to your life as a whole. Equally, it can be applied to organizations or units.

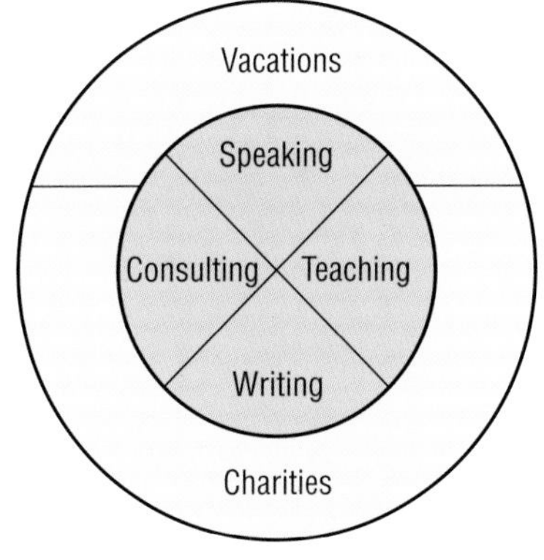

Handy's personal doughnut

At the core of Handy's doughnut are the various types of fee work to which he devotes about 200 days a year. In the outer space he has placed his charity work, which takes up approximately 100 days, and vacations, which claim 65 days a year.

Drawing your doughnut

Draw your personal version of the Handy doughnut. Place inside the doughnut your core activities – the tasks you must complete to earn a living and fulfill your career ambitions. The space around the core is where you place your other activities, the voluntary ones, the outside interests, the family, and so on. Now consider your personal doughnut. Is your life all core, or duty, and no personal space, or vice versa? Most people, says Handy, seem to like a balanced doughnut with about equal amounts of core and space.

Consider your work life, too. How much discretion do you have? Is your work doughnut all core – specific duties to perform – and no space for individual responsibility? Or do you work for an organization that gives individuals space outside the core in which to take initiatives and develop their strengths?

Creating your ideal

The principle of balance is well understood by people. Modern trends are making it much easier to obtain what you want at work – which is much more than money. When 2,000 employees were asked what mattered most in their work, the results showed clearly the greater importance of other factors.

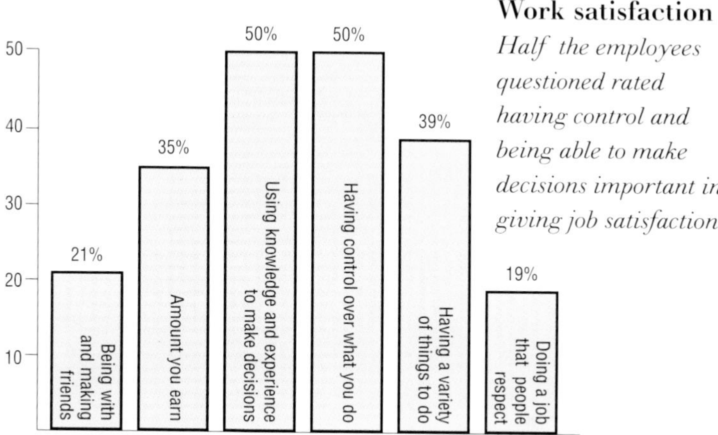

Work satisfaction
Half the employees questioned rated having control and being able to make decisions important in giving job satisfaction.

The portfolio career, in which you have several clients instead of one employer, provides the three prime needs in abundance. You may now be able to develop a portfolio career inside an organization: say, holding simultaneously a management role, a task-force function, and a planning position. That may well be an attractive option.

Optimizing your portfolio

You have an obligation to yourself to maximize your earning power. The portfolio career is a one-person company, and must be run efficiently. Work to a business plan that will generate a satisfactory financial return. Proper planning will almost certainly reveal gaps where you need new clients or more business from old ones. To win extra business, you will need to devote unpaid time to marketing.

You must also find unpaid time for education. Learning does not belong exclusively to your school days – it is important throughout your life. What you know represents your intellectual capital, the crucial asset. You must keep that capital in excellent condition.

2 Achieving excellence

Inside or outside an organization, if your results fail to satisfy an employer, insecurity will follow. Outside, whatever the quality of your work, continued employment is never guaranteed. Excellence is still the only insurance policy you can (and must) take out.

Playing to strengths

Achieving excellence is much easier if you are using your best talents, much harder if you are working in areas of weakness. Write down what you consider to be your best qualities and skills, and have them checked by somebody you can trust to be impartial and honest. Then make sure that your strengths match the work you plan to undertake. For example, do not become an independent consultant if you are shy or hesitant about selling yourself.

Learning to improve

Seek always to overcome your weaknesses and enhance your strengths by education and practice, by learning. That is where you not only maintain your intellectual capital, but expand it. Handy regards the learning process as having four parts:

- What is the question (problem to be solved, dilemma to be resolved, challenge to meet)?
- What are the possible answers?
- What does testing the possibilities tell me?
- What have I learned (reflection)?

This process neatly matches the PDCA approach to total quality management: Plan, Do, Check, Act.

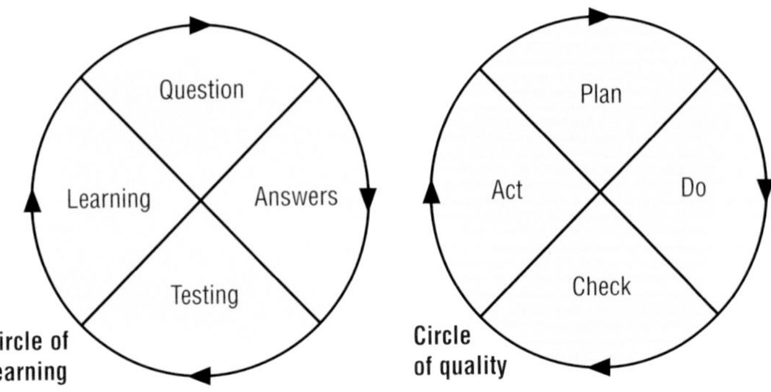

Supplying total quality

Use the PDCA process systematically to rethink and improve everything you do. Some of these improvements will be known only to you, like, say, meeting a standard of replying to all letters, e-mails, faxes, and phone calls on the day of receipt. Others will be all too obvious to the client, like delivering the work at the promised time. Set your standards at the highest level, and debrief clients on their assessment of your work – preferably face-to-face. That gives you the ultimate quality control and strengthens the relationship.

Going digital

Mastering the latest information technology will both enhance your efficiency and improve your communication with and service to clients. It will also help you manage your time more efficiently.

Master New Technology
Use a word-processing program to generate all documents.
Use a presentation program to create slides and reports.
Use email to speed and record most communication.
Use a spreadsheet to keep accounts and plan financially.
Use a planner to keep track of appointments and deadlines.
Use a personal database to list and cross-reference contacts.
Use a scanner to help file everything digitally.
Build your own website as a marketing and communication tool – and make it interactive.

Sustaining excellence

Finally, sustaining excellence depends, not only on tools and techniques, but on having a long-term view. To achieve this, adhere to the following four rules recommended by Handy:

- Take responsibility for yourself and your future.
- Form a clear view of what you want that future to be.
- Determine to get that future.
- Believe that you can do so. You can.

GLOSSARY

"Asterisk": Exceptional situation where the rulebook has failed and instinct and speed are required to achieve results.
Apollonians: Natural bureaucrats who prefer rules, control, and order in their working lives over enterprise and operational freedom.
Athenians: People who like to work in task forces and similar groups with a high degree of directed autonomy.
Chinese Contract: Commercial agreement that provides both sides with benefits likely to be lasting.
Culture: An organization's way of doing things; what works for the organization and what does not.
Dionysians: Free-thinking, independent individualists who are much happier outside organizational life.
Doughnut: Division between central core of essential activities and optional ones. Applies both to lives and organizations.
Federalism: Organization driven by its main, autonomous units, which report to a small coordinating center.
Flexilives: Careers that consist of several different jobs and employers (see Portfolio career).
Gods of Management: Handy metaphor for cultures: Zeus/power, Apollo/role, Athena/task, Dionysus/individual.
Hijack: Sabotage of operations by small groups of workers who between them are capable of exercising "negative power."
Inside-out: Reversing the conventional logic to achieve breakthroughs in thinking (see Upside-down).
Portfolio career: Having several employers either for the same work or for a collection of activities.
Paradox: Self-contradiction, whose acceptance was found by Handy to be fundamental in life and management.
Shamrock Organization: One divided into professional core, subcontractors, and flexible labor force.
Sigmoid Curve: The shape of the organizational life cycle, which can be extended by timely action before it reaches the crest.
"Slack": Handy's term for waste and ineffectiveness, "the lurking cancer of organizations."
Telecommuters: Also known as networked employees. People who work at home, using technology to communicate with the organization.
Trinitarian: Also known as "third-angle" thinking, it adds an extra approach to resolving a conflict between two parties.
Triple I: Organization that uses intelligence, information, and ideas to add value.
Type 1 and 2 errors: Type 1 errors are doing things wrong; Type 2 errors are not doing the right things.
Upside-down: Reversing conventional logic to achieve breakthroughs in thinking (see Inside-out).
Vision: A strategy that is intelligent and understandable, but stretches people's imaginations.
Zeus: The father-figure leader, typically found among companies still dominated by a founding entrepreneur.

BIBLIOGRAPHY

Charles Handy's books have sold over a million copies around the world. His first, *Understanding Organizations*, first published in 1976, and now in its fourth edition, has become a standard textbook. He broke new ground with *Gods of Management* (1978), with its powerful delineation of the four main management cultures. In the best-selling *The Age of Unreason* (1989) he worked on a broader canvas: the implications for society, and for individuals, of the dramatic ways in which technology and economics are changing workplaces and lives. *The Empty Raincoat* (called *The Age of Paradox* in the US) is the 1994 sequel to *Unreason*, and was named by both *Fortune* and *Business Week* as one of the 10 best business books of the year.

Handy has won two McKinsey Awards for articles in the *Harvard Business Review* – "Balancing Corporate Power: A New Federalist Paper" (1992), and "Trust and the Virtual Organization" (1995). *Beyond Certainty*, a collection of Handy's articles and essays, was published in 1995, as was *Waiting for the Mountain to Move*, a collection of his radio "Thoughts" over 10 years. His *The Hungry Spirit* was published in September 1997. It explores and explains his doubts about some consequences of free-market capitalism and questions the validity of material success. Handy combined his skills with those of his wife Elizabeth, a portrait photographer, for the 1999 book *The New Alchemists* – a photographic and literary portrait of Londoners who have "created something out of nothing."

WORKS CITED

Charles Handy (1992) *Understanding Organizations*, Penguin, London
– (1995) *Gods of Management*, Arrow, London
– (1995) *The Age of Unreason*, Arrow, London
– (1995) *The Empty Raincoat*, Arrow, London
– (1995) *Beyond Certainty*, Arrow, London
– (1995) *Waiting for the Mountain to Move*, Arrow, London
– (1998) *The Hungry Spirit*, Arrow, London
– (1999) *The New Alchemists*, Hutchinson, London

Index

Page numbers in *italics* refer to picture captions.

CHARLES HANDY

Robert Heller

Robert Heller is himself a prolific author of management books. The first, *The Naked Manager*, published in 1972, established Heller as an iconoclastic, wide-ranging guide to managerial excellence – and incompetence. Heller has drawn on the extensive knowledge of managers and management he acquired as the founding editor of *Management Today*, Britain's premier business magazine, which he headed for 25 years. Books such as *The Supermanagers* and *In Search of European Excellence* address the ways in which the latest ideas on change, quality, and motivation are providing new routes to business success. In 1990 Heller wrote *Culture Shock*, one of the first books to describe how IT would revolutionize management. Since then, as writer, lecturer, and consultant, Heller has continued to tell managers how to "Ride the Revolution," the title of his 2000 book, written with Paul Spenley. His books for Dorling Kindersley's Essential Managers series are international bestsellers.